More praise for *Tropical Plants and How to Love Them:*

"Marianne never fails to inspire, educate, and entertain with her writing. *Tropical Plants and How to Love Them* is a joy from cover to cover. She speaks from experience, weaving humor and empathy with a love of tropicals while challenging readers to reconsider their relationships with the plants they hold dear."

— Dan Scott, Director of Horticulture, American Horticultural Society

"This is a book we need today more than ever. Marianne Willburn gives us practical advice on how to grow tropical plants outside and later enjoy inside as houseplants. She writes like a trusted friend giving you helpful dating advice, including how to find the best match and evaluate it for maintenance and long-term possibilities. Like any good dating site, the photos are important and hers are beautiful."

— R. William Thomas, Executive Director, Chanticleer Garden, USA

"I am really impressed with this book. It's accessible, inspirational, and packed full of excellent advice. I love the idea of categorizing plants in a practical, fun, and relatable way, and admired Marianne's decision to challenge many of the arbitrary divisions often trotted out in gardening books between houseplants and garden plants. It's sparked a renewed excitement about using tropical plants in my own garden and giving my houseplants a summer holiday outside too."

— Jane Perrone, garden writer and host of *On The Ledge* podcast

"Marianne has managed to make me fall in love with tropical planting even deeper than ever before. I feel full of inspiration and have so many new ideas for my tropical plantings here in Hunting Brook."

— Jimi Blake, Horticulturist, Hunting Brook Gardens, Ireland

"A delight to read such a comprehensive guide to my passion. Playfully written with inspirational images and accessible practical advice that will encourage the reader to experiment themselves. I particularly enjoyed the guilt-free Summer Romance plants, mocktrops, and the entertaining plant relationship guidance."

— Emma Allen, Garden Manager, Glasshouse and Exotic Garden, RHS Garden Wisley, UK

"In *Tropical Plants and How to Love Them*, Marianne shows temperate gardeners they need not strictly relegate tropical plants to windowsills. Instead, she coaxes us outdoors and demonstrates how to practically use them to grace our garden beds, containers, and water gardens. Whether it's a dramatic Canna lily or a colorful coleus, Marianne covers a range of common and not-so-common plants that will undoubtedly give any garden a 'wow' factor."

— Summer Rayne Oakes, author of *How to Make a Plant Love You* and host of *Plant One On Me*

"The more I read, the more I wanted to stop reading and drive immediately to my local garden center! Marianne's passion for these plants is contagious, and her expertise will undoubtedly inspire a new generation of 'tropical' gardeners. *Tropical Plants and How to Love Them* is full of inspiring plant combinations, gorgeous photographs, and excellent technical advice. I'm ready to plant!"

— Ellen Zachos, author of *Tempting Tropicals* and co-host of *Plantrama* podcast

"*Tropical Plants and How to Love Them* is fantastic! I love the layout, I love the premise, and I love the little stories that each chapter creates."

— Dan Benarcik, Horticulturist, Chanticleer Garden, USA

Marianne Willburn

TROPICAL PLANTS

AND HOW TO LOVE THEM

Building a Relationship with Heat-Loving Plants
WHEN YOU DON'T LIVE IN THE TROPICS

COOL
SPRINGS
PRESS

Brimming with creative inspiration, how-to projects, and useful information to enrich your everyday life, Quarto Knows is a favorite destination for those pursuing their interests and passions. Visit our site and dig deeper with our books into your area of interest: Quarto Creates, Quarto Cooks, Quarto Homes, Quarto Lives, Quarto Drives, Quarto Explores, Quarto Gifts, or Quarto Kids.

First Published in 2021 by Cool Springs Press, an imprint of The Quarto Group,
100 Cummings Center, Suite 265-D, Beverly, MA 01915, USA.
T (978) 282-9590 F (978) 283-2742 QuartoKnows.com

Cool Springs Press titles are also available at discount for retail, wholesale, promotional, and bulk purchase. For details, contact the Special Sales Manager by email at specialsales@quarto.com or by mail at The Quarto Group, Attn: Special Sales Manager, 100 Cummings Center, Suite 265-D, Beverly, MA 01915, USA.

25 24 23 22 21   1 2 3 4 5

ISBN: 978-0-7603-6894-7

Digital edition published in 2021

Library of Congress Control Number 2020949495

Design and Page Layout: Amy Sly
Photography: Marianne Willburn, except where noted, and Shutterstock.com
   on pages 182 (bottom), 195 (top left)
Illustration: Holly Neel

Printed in China

To my husband Michael,
who lives with a lot of plants
and never complains when I add another

contents

Introduction

Fifteen years ago, I didn't use tropical plants in my garden—at least most of those that you will find within the pages of this book. I didn't particularly care for them. I could appreciate and enjoy the romance of a tropical garden in a tropical setting, but bringing those elements into my own mid-Atlantic garden seemed an expensive, labor-intensive, and incongruous way of gardening when there were excellent plants available fully suited to my climate.

This may have had much to do with the quality and diversity of the plant available at my local garden centers.

Thirsty canna lilies too big for their plastic pots and the odd, ragged bird of paradise on summer racks did not make a convincing case for putting tropical accents in my garden.

Neither did the price. I have always watched my pennies carefully and seed-reared most of my own annuals. If I would not spend fifteen bucks on a flat of pretty pansies, I wasn't going to blow it on one, tired-looking tropical plant that would perish at the end of the season.

And then I fell in love.

It's difficult to describe what happened any better.

It Happened One Night. Well, One Day, Anyway.

The month was July. I was visiting friends and their gardens in North Carolina, and the weather was hot and muggy. And in traditional planting schemes featuring old favorites such as *Hydrangea* and *Hosta*, there stood an extraordinary burst of chartreuse foliage in the form of an elephant ear cultivar named 'Lime Zinger' (*Xanthosoma aurea*). It did not dominate the bed, but gave it depth and vigor, and complemented the plants growing nearby.

In another area of the garden *Canna* 'Bengal Tiger' was performing a similar miracle—adding contrast, form, and excitement to the garden without expending a single bloom.

I was instantly smitten, but—like the best love affairs—moving slowly. I asked for, and was generously granted, a division of both plants. On the way home I visited a favorite haunt—Plant Delights Nursery, just outside Raleigh, North Carolina. For the first time perhaps, I knew what tropical and subtropical plants were adding to the display gardens—because I was specifically paying attention to those elements of the design.

My little divisions did well for the rest of the summer. By autumn they had multiplied, so I made an "insurance division" of each to keep in the house with me, and stored the rest in the basement without care—just as I had been told to do. At the end of the winter, all four were alive and healthy and they went back into the garden as soon as temperatures would support them.

All summer long I marveled at the impact they made—particularly when contrasting them with other temperate plants that stumbled in the heat. When deep orange blooms appeared on the canna lily, they were icing on the cake. When hummingbirds arrived and fought over the blooms, I wondered why I had allowed myself to be so prejudiced for so long.

Xanthosoma aurea 'Lime Zinger' brings a touch of sunlight to a shady, temperate bed.

Relationships Develop

I experimented with more genera. I had to search, but not as much as I might have done twenty years before. Luckily for me, advances in propagation were making it easier to find plants that might have required a second mortgage in the past.

As my passion grew over those years of exposure to new plant material, I recognized that their overwintering requirements did not need to be approached in the same way, and I thought of these exciting plants in terms of four relationship types: the Summer Romance, the Long-Term Commitment, the Best Friend, and the High-Maintenance Partner, and a bonus relationship—Friends with Benefits.

Some explanation is obviously necessary . . .

The bold colors and patterns of tropical foliage can make quite an impact in a temperate garden. Here in the author's garden, *Ricinus communis* (castor bean), *Manihot esculenta* 'Variegata' (variegated tapioca) and Canna 'Bengal Tiger', inject vibrant color without expending a single bloom.

The Summer Romance

Tropical plants you fall in love with and enjoy during the growing season, but kiss good-bye when summer ends.

I realized that it was okay to let an exciting tropical plant perish at the end of a long spring and summer on the deck; and that the cost was far below the incredible value it brought to my outside life.

It's okay to allow a sumptuous summer combo light up your world for just a season. Pictured: *Syngonium podophyllum* 'Holly.'

The Best Friend

Tropical plants that don't need a greenhouse, living room, or pampering to overwinter in a dormant state.

I embraced those tropical plants that made things even easier by going fully dormant in a frost-free basement or garage.

Luxurious *Canna* foliage unfurls in the summer garden. In autumn, the rhizomes will be stored with little ceremony in a dark garage.

Friends with Benefits

Tropical plants that enhance our gardens while also providing edible or medicinal value.

I learned which plants I could use in the kitchen, and I didn't have to stress when the season was over and the plant died, any more than I stressed over a tomato plant.

Young ginger rhizomes, harvested and ready to slice for pickling

The Long-Term Commitment

Tropical plants that make your outdoor spaces shine in the summer, and then double as gorgeous houseplants over the winter months.

I easily committed to plants that functioned as excellent, sturdy houseplants over the winter, after they'd spent months beautifying the garden in summer.

The common houseplant devil's ivy (*Epipremnum aureus*) creates a lush groundcover in summer.

The High-Maintenance Partner

Tropical plants that expect a lot. But we do it for them because we love them. For now.

I would find myself tempted by the occasional tropical plant that said "pamper me." And lovesick and besotted, I would. Right until the moment I wouldn't any longer.

A red pineapple is one of the more tempting High-Maintenance Partners. But how long will you cope with a spiny three-footer in your bathroom?

What Is a Temperate Garden?

Temperate gardeners are seasonal gardeners. A *temperate* climate is characterized by significant seasonal differences and temperature variations throughout the year. Generally, these are the climate zones on either side of the equator that fall between the subtropics and their corresponding polar region—approximately 35 to 66 degrees north and south. Often, subpolar regions are additionally excluded, defining temperate as the latitudes between 35 and 50 degrees north and south.

And when I spoke to temperate gardening groups about tropical plants using these terms, I found that they resonated.

Temperate gardeners—even experienced ones—can feel overwhelmed by the idea of using tropical plants. They don't want to kill them, but they don't necessarily want to live with them forever either. So, they never start, even when they're sorely tempted.

Categorizing these plants into five memorable relationship types that gardeners could recognize and change according to their own lives and the plants they loved made many gardeners more willing to experiment—whether for a season, for a year, or for decades.

But Relationships Can Change

More than ten years after I began my tropical journey, my garden is not a tropical garden. It is a temperate garden accented by the color, contrast, and vigor of tropical plants—in beds, in containers, on shady patios, and on sunny decks—particularly during the difficult summer months.

They serve in different functions: In some beds they might provide structure. In others, a feeling of lush abundance. In all, however, there is novelty and excitement.

Each autumn, I dig some plants and I let some perish. Others I carefully treat for pests and bring indoors to serve as stunning houseplants over the winter months. The time I spend doing this is variable, and directly linked to four factors:

1. my mood

2. my energy

3. my time; and,

4. my history with a specific plant.

Those relationships could change tomorrow. They *will* change tomorrow. And that's what this book is about—falling in love with the remarkable qualities that tropical plants can bring to your temperate garden; and giving yourself permission to let that relationship develop and evolve.

On your terms.

above and right The garden is always color-forward when tropical foliage gets involved.

Defining Tropical

You have most likely grown tropical and subtropical plants without ever knowing it—coleus, *Lantana*, and impatiens are just a few popular examples. One or two of these are represented in this book, but for the most part, the plants you'll find within these pages softly whisper "tropical."

Tropical is a feeling we all recognize when we see, smell, or taste it: large leaves, bright colors, warm days. But the true definition of tropical is a little more specific.

Tropical plants are those plants considered native to latitudes between the Tropic of Cancer and the Tropic of Capricorn (approximately 23.5 degrees north and south of the equator, respectively). Though growing conditions can vary by elevation, terrain, and prevailing weather patterns, these plants benefit from a climate with relatively constant day length, high average humidity and annual temperatures, and the absence of killing frosts. High average rainfalls are also common throughout the tropics.

Not all tropical plants are sun lovers—many are plants from the forest understory and will happily live in the low-light conditions of your shady deck or home.

Many of the tropical plants we buy are actually *subtropical*—they are native to regions in the geographical band between the tropics and the beginning of temperate climates. These regions experience infrequent frosts and can be just as dry as they are wet. Temperate gardeners often have a little more leeway with these plants: leaves can be hit by light early frost and be fine, but will be left browned and devastated by a hard freeze.

For this book, and the ease of the reader, I refer to tropical and subtropical plants broadly as tropicals. The most important take-away for you as a temperate gardener is that very few of these plants are naturally winter hardy to a temperate climate, and you must take action to keep them alive when autumn frosts fall.

Musa basjoo (the hardy banana) is one of the rare tropical plants that can be mulched heavily and survive temperatures down to -10°F (-23°C). This clump sits outside my second-story office, and by the end of the season the wide, lush leaves are brushing the windows.

Why Grow Tropical Plants?

As temperate gardeners, we have a leg up on our tropical cousins. We can combine the best of their gardens with the best of ours. We can grow a cool-season lilac, and then hide those unattractive legs with a potted *Schefflera* during the summer, allowing this popular houseplant to do double-duty inside when temperatures drop.

It's not so easy the other way around, as those who have tried to grow a lilac in Florida can tell you.

Used cleverly, tropical plants can:

- Give you star power during the hot, often humid days of summer and early autumn.

- Accentuate water features or accentuate wetter areas in the garden.

- Add an unusual element to traditional plantings.

- Create a themed tropical garden.

- Create a sense of enclosure and privacy on decks and patios.

- Thrill your taste buds with fresh, unusual flavors.

- Create a lush indoor garden.

- Allow you to experiment with exotic plants that, by virtue of their hardiness, won't become an invasive threat in your garden.[1]

---

[1] Regions of course vary, and some of the tropical and subtropical plants you use may be hardy in your garden. Before using a plant with exotic origins, especially near waterways, consult your region's agricultural service.

How Should You Use This Book?

Tropical Plants and How to Love Them is intended to guide gardeners in temperate climates who are new to tropical plants, those who have dabbled and want more suggestions, or those interested in using their houseplants in creative outdoor ways. It's for those who want the cold hard truth about what you may have to do to get that banana through the winter, or could use a little absolution for treating an expensive *Alcantarea* like an annual *Petunia*.

Each relationship type has a chapter dedicated to it in the first section to explain what makes a good candidate for each category. Specific plants are cited to illustrate the relationship, and where necessary, general overwintering processes are described to help you understand what may be required of you. We'll start with the easiest one—the Summer Romance—and gradually get more challenging.

The second section is about actually *using* them. How do we take these bold, breathtaking plants and incorporate them smoothly into our traditional temperate gardens? What if we are battling a challenging climate? Chapter 6 will help you answer these questions, and get you using tropicals like a pro. You'll also learn more about Mocktrops—plants that give off a tropical vibe but are remarkably hardy outdoors.

The third section is all about the plants. Profiles of both common and uncommon tropical plants are provided in these pages, listed by their botanical name. This selection is far from comprehensive, but it is intended to give those either new to tropicals (or a few years into their journey) good suggestions for taking things up a notch.

I have used icons throughout the book for each genus's primary relationship. Those same icons will help you identify which plants also make fabulous Friends with Benefits—flavoring your favorite exotic dishes while they flavor your garden with exotic textures.

The decision of how to treat a plant is extremely personal. My Summer Romance might tempt another gardener to treat it as High-Maintenance Partner—but an even more obsessed plant-hound will wonder what all the fuss is about and consider the upkeep a reasonable part of a Long-Term Commitment.

It is more important to understand *the reasons behind those decisions* rather than the decisions themselves, so you can make them in your own garden based upon your own needs.

So, relax. You will not find a 500-word treatise on the ovarian differences between *Colocasia* and *Alocasia* within these pages. What you will find is joy in this incredible palette of plants—a celebration of their diversity and a grateful appreciation of the excitement they can bring to a temperate garden.

A gorgeous selection of bromeliads and *Tradescantia*. (Mountsier Garden, Nutley, New Jersey).

THE
RELATIONSHIP

The Summer Romance

Sexy. Exciting. Fleeting.

Summer Romances happen when you least expect them. One moment you're selecting respectable foundation shrubs at your favorite garden center—the next, your eyes are caught by the deep pink blossoms and shiny, variegated foliage of a giant *Mandevilla* snaking up a trellis a few feet away.

You know you're being played—that it won't be a long-term thing—but you can't help yourself. Pot goes in cart, money is exchanged, Partner grumbles. Once home, it's the first thing out of the car and onto the deck—where it practically mixes the rum punches for dinner parties and makes you grin all season long.

But four months later you recognize that things are changing. Pumpkin lattés have replaced summer cocktails, and you begin to naturally disconnect from the plant that brought so much to your late spring and summer season.

Soon the first frost will wilt foliage and flower. The tender, tropical *Mandevilla* must come inside or perish.

Perhaps you feel a twinge of guilt, but then you remember your great-aunt's winter windowsills, stuffed to capacity with sad, struggling plants that desperately needed an editing.

You are strengthened by this memory. You are in control. There is a season for everything and it's time to say good-bye.

> Tropical plants say "vacation" even when it's just another workday.

Every season must end, and many of our best romances will fade into memory. Next year there'll be new adventures and new plant combinations to be had. Let go and have a latté.

Yes, this beautiful Summer Romance is over, but who knows what will catch your eye at the garden center next spring. Summer Romances are meant to be guilt-free and exciting. Let yourself indulge.

There aren't too many rules—just guidelines for knowing when to let go.

FIRST, LET GO OF THE GUILT

Plants die. It's okay.

I still have to remind myself of this maxim, even though I have heard it countless times.

Most of us have limited space. If none of the plants we grew died, our experience with growing plants would be just as limited.

The compulsion to save a plant runs deep in a gardener's psyche, and it is a worthy one. Frugality and future availability of a plant also play a role. Whether it's a succulent jade leaf you picked up off the sidewalk that you know you can root in a little damp sand, or a friend's abused *Philodendron* that you miraculously brought back to life, rescuing a plant takes a bit of skill and makes us feel good about ourselves as gardeners. Conversely, letting a plant die feels like giving up.

But should it?

Some of the very same gardeners that will rescue that *Philodendron* think nothing of treating a large pot of coleus as an annual at the end of the summer. But some species of coleus (*Plectranthus scutellarioides*) are evergreen perennials in frost-free regions, and fully capable of living a lot longer than four months.

The difference is the *Philodendron* has traditionally been marketed to cool-climate gardeners as a houseplant and the coleus has been marketed as an annual. Thus, we are trained to think about these vigorous plants differently and to value them differently.

EVERY PLANT HAS A FUNCTION

There is yet another aspect of a plant we should consider: the *function* those plants are performing in our lives and our landscapes. If the function of a plant is to bring seasonal excitement and color to our decks, our patios, our gardens, and our balconies—but they cannot survive the winter outdoors or perform that same function indoors—why can't we grow them as annuals?

Bottom line: I'm asking you to retrain your brain when it comes to plants that make more sense to grow for a season than to hold onto forever. I (and countless other industry professionals) am giving you permission to have a guilt-free summer romance with a sexy, stunning plant.

And to do it again next year.

Lantana may look strong and structural, but it cannot withstand cold winters. If you don't want to dig it, wrap it, and store it—let it go.

Coleus and *Alternanthera* make a beautiful, but temporary, pairing for the growing season. You can take tip cuttings of both in the autumn—but you must ask yourself, "Do I really want to?"

23

The summer season is all about indulging.

What Kind of Plant Makes a Good Summer Romance?

Overwintering a tender plant is a personal decision and can change from year to year. When deciding to spend a winter together, consider whether your tropical plant:

NEEDS STRONG SUNLIGHT AND GOOD HUMIDITY LEVELS ALL YEAR LONG
If we're constantly slathering lotion on dry, cracked skin during the winter months, and feeling our mood lift when the sun shines, you can imagine how plants feel.

Though some tropical plants can adapt well to low light levels, spotty care, and dry air for a season and still look great (such as Long-Term Commitments *Peperomia* or *Philodendron*), others, such as a banana, will succumb to pests or disease and are better treated as a Summer Romance; or, if the love affair unexpectedly takes you deeper, as a High-Maintenance Partner.

This red Abyssinian banana cost less than a bouquet of cut flowers but has put on 5 feet (1.5 m) of growth in one season. If saving it feels like a hassle, you won't be losing much of an investment for five months of fun.

HAS A TENDENCY TO SHED A LOT OF BLOSSOMS OR LEAVES

Are you house-proud? Unless a plant is unusually messy, we rarely notice how much it is shedding during the growing season. As soon as it comes indoors and a vacuum gets involved, we pay attention.

Many plants (particularly ferns and some species of *Ficus*) respond to poor conditions by losing even more foliage—all over your taupe sofa or pristine carpet. If they are otherwise adding a lot to the décor like a flowering crown of thorns (*Euphorbia milii*), you may put up with it. If they're struggling, this may be the last straw.

NEEDS A LONG GROWING SEASON OR SEVERAL GROWING SEASONS TO FRUIT OR FLOWER

Often it's the flower or the fruit that encourages us to make an impulse purchase. Orchids and ornamental pineapples are an example of this.

These plants have been given long growing seasons (sometimes several) by expert growers to get them to the point where you grab them off the shelf with your heart pounding. Everyday gardeners are unlikely to repeat those conditions without a fair amount of effort. In the case of once-fruiting pineapples, you must wait for offspring to start the process again.

IS A WATER PLANT, OR A PLANT WITH HIGH WATER REQUIREMENTS

Water plants such as papyrus (*Cyperus*), water hyacinth (*Eichhornia crassipes*), and tropical species of water lilies (*Nymphaea*) are plants that also enjoy high levels of sunlight. Unless you've got a large indoor water feature in your home, you are unlikely to give them what they need without a lot of mess, hassle, and general grumpiness.

IS CONSTANTLY PLAGUED BY INDOOR PESTS

Pests are opportunistic, and their favorite opportunity is a plant that's struggling. Some tropical plants suffer indoor insects more than others, and therefore make better Summer Romances than Long-Term Commitments.

For instance, bananas are always on a spider mite's menu. It's a pest that loves dry conditions in both the garden and the home and will quickly injure and disfigure a banana's delicate large leaves.

Owning a greenhouse is no guarantee against problems when it comes to rapidly growing tropical plants.

GETS TOO BIG DURING THE GROWING SEASON TO COMFORTABLY LIVE WITH INDOORS

If you've never overwintered a 10-foot (3 m) banana with 8-foot (2.4 m) ceilings, you'll only try it once.

IS RELATIVELY CHEAP AND/OR EASY TO REPLACE

The price of tropical plants has decreased in recent years thanks to the science behind tissue culture, a process that rapidly clones tropical and temperate plants in laboratories. Consequently, propagators do not necessarily need to divide plants, wait for "pups," or take limited cuttings from stock plants in order to sell to growers and retailers. Where it may have made sense in the past to overwinter a special bromeliad, the gardener can now take advantage of greater selection and online availability season after season.

Water lettuce (*Pistia stratiotes*) as a pond playground for happy frogs. But perhaps not in your living room.

Naranjilla seeds (*Solanum quitoense*) drying on a paper towel at the end of the season for next year's Summer Romances

Papaya grown from a seed in early spring can bring incredible Summer Romance structure to a garden bed. (Chanticleer Garden, Wayne, Pennsylvania)

CAN BE RAISED AND ENJOYED FROM SEED IN EARLY SPRING

Some tropical plants are natural Summer Romances because they are just so darn easy to start from seed and they grow so vigorously during the summer months.

Castor bean (*Ricinus communis*), papaya (*Carica papaya*), and naranjilla (*Solanum quitoense*) are good examples of vigorous "annual" tropical plants that give you a whole lot of bang for your buck and won't guilt you into keeping them through the winter any more than your pepper plant does.

Depending on the length of your season, some will fruit and some will not. Plant naranjilla seed in early spring indoors and by the end of the growing season, you'll not only benefit from the unique texture of the fuzzy, thorned leaves, but you'll also have little orange fruits you can use to flavor ice cream or cocktails.

Papaya needs a long tropical season to create those characteristic large fruits, but one little seed from a grocery store fruit can grow to give you large fascinating foliage and a structural tree 15+ feet (4.6 m) tall in just a season. That's value for money!

CAN BE *ANY* PLANT, NO MATTER HOW WELL BEHAVED OR EASY TO CARE FOR

It just depends on what you're looking for and how you're feeling this year.

What Is Tissue Culture Anyway?

Vegetatively propagated plants often arrive at independent garden centers as liners—an industry term for juvenile plants that will need an additional eight to ten weeks of care to create the stunning plant you will eventually fall for. Many of these liners—both temperate and tropical species—are now propagated through tissue culture.

Gardeners familiar with traditional methods of asexual propagation—division, cuttings, layering, etc. . . . are also very aware of how much time it can take to get a new plant healthy and rooted—even in a greenhouse setting. That propagation process has been accelerated by the laboratory-based science of tissue culture, which went mainstream in the early 1980s. For the consumer, this means greater availability and selection at the garden center and often at a lesser cost. A friend and horticulturist jokes that, before tissue culture took off, he had to give plasma to get his hands on the tropical plants he wanted.

New plants are created from a 2 to 4 mm section of a plant's growing point initiated from a main or side shoot. The material is sterilized and placed in a 6½ ounce (192 ml) jar, and within four weeks—in a 78°F (26°C) environment with fourteen hours of light a day—leaves have formed. In twelve weeks, six to eight unrooted baby plants are ready to be divided into new jars, and so on

and so on . . . "It's accelerated multiplication," says Mike Rinck, president of AG3, Inc, a tissue culture lab in Florida, USA.

The growing solution is then changed to allow the juvenile plants to root, and the last stage of the process is transitioning a plant to soil—a plant that has only known the perfection of laboratory conditions.

Both temperate herbaceous perennials and tropical plants are propagated using this labor-intensive process, but it is not without its difficulties. Different plants require different solution recipes, naturally occurring mutations can be accelerated right along with growth, and everything must be kept 100 percent sterile.

Traditional methods of propagation are far from being phased out. But this fascinating process has significantly improved consumer access to a wealth of tropical plant material. In short, making it a lot easier to have a summer fling.

Seed-Rearing Tropical Annuals

Some of our easiest and most guilt-free Summer Romances are plants we can grow from seed early in the season. It's possible to invest very little money and yet enjoy a plant that puts on remarkable growth and adds an unusual, often very colorful, touch to the garden. If you're having a hard time finding a rare species, this may be the way to go.

Sourcing tropical seeds has become much easier as tropicals become more mainstream; but you shouldn't make assumptions when sowing them. Follow the packet instructions carefully, recognizing that many have higher heat and humidity requirements for germination. Some need scarification (nicking the seed coat), or like castor bean or black-eyed Susan vine (*Thunbergia alata*), benefit greatly from a twenty-four-hour soaking.

Whether you plant directly in the ground or indirectly in pots is a personal preference and somewhat dependent on the conditions and pests of your garden. I indirectly sow seed in pots so I can keep track of seedlings in a big garden and give them a head start on the season with lots of heat and moisture; but I always smile to see the occasional self-seeded castor beans germinating in early summer—often besting their cold-frame cousins. Do not get started too early if you cannot maintain a warm, moist environment. Many tropical seeds will simply rot.

SOME HIGHLY ORNAMENTAL TROPICAL PLANTS THAT GROW WELL FROM SEED:

- Naranjilla (*Solanum quitoense*)
- Castor bean (*Ricinus communis*)
- Black-eyed Susan vine (*Thunbergia alata*)
- Papaya (*Carica papaya*)
- Red okra 'Candle Fire' (*Abelmoschus esculentus*)
- Striped Japonica corn 'Field of Dreams' (*Zea mays*)
- Spider flower (*Cleome hassleriana*)
- Red roselle (*Hibiscus sabdariffa*)
- Purple hyacinth bean (*Lablab purpureus*)
- Four o'clocks (*Mirabilis jalapa*)
- Coral plant (*Jatropha multifida*)
- Candle bush (*Senna alata*)
- Malabar spinach (*Basella rubra*)
- Cranberry hibiscus (*Hibiscus acetosella*)
- Cup-and-saucer vine (*Cobaea scandens*)
- Tall verbena (*Verbena bonariensis*)
- Rattlebox (*Crotalaria spectabilis*)
- Dahlia (*Dahlia* spp.)

With moisture and rich soil, tropical seedlings will quickly create stunning combinations in your temperate garden. Here, black-eyed Susan vine (*Thunbergia alata*) with the ornamental patio peach 'Bonfire.'

Don't Forget About *Your Needs*

It takes two to make a relationship work. If you're truthful with yourself from the beginning, you won't end up feeling guilty over things that were destined to happen.

The best way of doing this is by examining past behaviors and making decisions based on those, *not* the superhuman you're sure you'll turn into just as soon as you buy this change-your-life ficus.

There are no right or wrong answers. I have a good friend who owns a nursery, propagates plants like a diva, and can grow anything under the sun. Her blood probably runs green. Yet she doesn't own a single houseplant. She doesn't have time for them and would rather save that space for something else. And she happily admits it.

Know your truth. It'll save you a lot of stress in the long run.

So, are you a person who:

HAS LIMITED INDOOR SPACE?

Even the tiniest homes can showcase thriving houseplants, but they may not have visual room for High-Maintenance Partners that look terrible over the winter. It's better to choose those that do well indoors—enhancing, not detracting from, your home's interior—and discard the rest at the end of the season.

HAS LIMITED OUTDOOR SPACE?

When the season starts, we want a beautiful patio space and gorgeous plants creating a certain mood. If you don't have outside room for a holding area or cold frames where your plants can bulk up, it makes more sense to go shopping for some Summer Romance instant impact as soon as the season begins, and let a professional grower do the hard (and expensive!) work.

TRAVELS A GREAT DEAL?

Plants need regular care, just like pets, and some tropical plants will not cope well with being ignored for a week or more. If you travel often during the winter months, it's best to let your Summer Romances end when the frost begins to settle.

HAS SEVERAL INDOOR PETS?

Pets love plants. Between the dogs chasing each other behind the *Schefflera* and breaking branches, or the cats using the papyrus as their personal vegetable stand and adjoining restroom, winter months can become a little tense. You also don't want to take chances on poisoning your pets with exotic foliage. If it all seems a little much, it's time for a Summer Romance instead.

FINDS HOUSEPLANTS CLUTTERING?

I'm not a minimalist, but I do admit to a certain feeling of relief once the tropical houseplants have been herded (sometimes thrown) outdoors in the late spring. If you don't particularly like houseplants, or like them only as architectural or decorative accents, you may find that over-wintering all of your tropical purchases is too cluttering.

Castor bean, striped Japonica corn, and red okra seedlings share space with *Cosmos* and sunflowers in a temporary straw bale cold frame.

A Message to Frugal Gardeners

Frugal gardeners reading the above may scream "But what about the MONEY!" to an inanimate book and its obviously profligate author.

I hear you. I have spent most of my gardening life trying to figure out how to make more from less, much from something, and anything from nothing.

In many ways, that's why I got into tropical plants. They were not only beautiful, but some (such as *Canna* and *Colocasia*) grew and reproduced themselves so vigorously with so little work that even new garden beds suddenly looked as if I'd spent a lot of money on them. If you are trying to

save money, the best way to begin with tropical plants is with your Best Friends.

That said, my time, effort, and energy are forms of currency in my world, and no doubt, in yours. If I spend inordinate amounts of any of those things on something I can spend a reasonable amount to replace, I consider it money well spent, plus I help local garden centers in the process by supporting their growing efforts.

"Reasonable" is a relative term—not only between households, but within our own household at different times in our lives. And we must decide for ourselves.

Saying Good-bye

It's very difficult to get rid of plants that have been beautiful over the season, especially when you know that you might buy them again next year.

Here are some thoughts to motivate you if you are finding it particularly hard to end a Summer Romance:

- Think about how good you feel after having a good clear-out of clothes, books, tools, furniture, and other miscellany you never thought you could part with. Turns out you could.

- Reflect for a moment on the windowsills of your most die-hard plant-geek friend. Do you want those windowsills?

- Think about your pepper plants—or your petunias. You could keep these subtropical beauties alive indoors over the winter, but you happily use them as summer annuals. Expand your definition of an annual.

Now, here are practical ways of making the split less painful:

- If they are in containers, don't let them die in place, where you'll look at those brown stems throughout the winter and feel guilty. Replace them with winter ornamentals such as purple kale, *Carex*, pansies, or twigs of yellow or red dogwood.

- Place your plants on a compost pile or *hügelkultur* mound, where they can break down and enrich the soil for future plants. Throw some straw over them to make it easier on both of you. Well . . . on you at least.

- Ask friends if they would like to give them a home. Some people are happy to throw them in a greenhouse or baby them over the winter. Nearing the end of the season, give friends a cut-off date and if they haven't picked them up by then—compost them.

- Bring your plants to a fall plant swap, where more collectors are usually present and the overflow goes into the host's garden, greenhouse, or compost pile. Label them "tender" for beginning gardeners who might not know what they are looking at.

Before consigning your plant to the compost pile, you can often take cuttings and root them for new spring plants (such as *Alternanthera*, coleus, or shrimp plant), but we'll deal with that in the High-Maintenance Partner chapter later (chapter 4). Even easily rooted cuttings take care and attention, and right now we're talking about letting go!

Finding the One . . . Or Several of Them

Sometimes a Summer Romance gets serious.

As a temperate gardener playing with tropical plants, you're bound to fall hard every once in a while and fight to keep what you have loved for a season.

You'll have three relationship choices going forward, and it may not be clear at the beginning if you're taking on a Long-Term Commitment, a High-Maintenance Partner, or a Best Friend.

The following chapters and plant profiles will guide you in that determination, but I must re-emphasize that one person's Long-Term Commitment will be another's High-Maintenance Partner.

After taking their relationship to the next level, some gardeners might even decide that the no-strings-attached Summer Romance worked much better for everyone involved.

In short, it's personal. I have no desire to micromanage storage temperatures for picky *Caladium* bulbs, but every fall, you'll find me digging and carting 4 x 50 pounds (22.7 kg) worth of red Abyssinian banana (*Ensete ventricosum 'Maurelii'*) into my garage. How does that make sense?

I'm in love and love doesn't make sense. But you may not be as banana-besotted as I am, and instead put your efforts into keeping those *Caladium* bulbs happy, or maintaining a windowsill of *Alternanthera* cuttings.

So, are you ready to take it to the next level? Let's start with the relationship that's built upon two happy partners: Tropical plants that look great indoors and gardeners who love houseplants.

I'm talking about a Long-Term Commitment.

A bath every week or two is all that air plants (*Tillandsia*) need to get through the winter, making them terrific Long-Term Commitments in busy lives. But this could be too much for your level of busy.

A gorgeous sea of *Caladium* seamlessly melds with *Alpinia* and *Acalypha* in the Mountsier Garden in Nutley, New Jersey. These *Caladium* will be treated as beautiful Summer Romances and enjoyed right up to the first frosts of autumn.

Using Botanical Names

Let's talk botanical names. I know some of you don't want to, but please bear with me for a moment—one gardener to another. It's important.

Having stood on both sides of this fence in my life (intimidated vs. knowledgeable), I can confidently say that the time you take to become familiar with the *real* names of your plants—even on a (literal) generic basis—will help you as a gardener in three major ways:

Cultivation: Elephant ears are elephant ears, right? Wrong. Elephant ears can be *Alocasia*, *Colocasia*, *Xanthosoma*, *Caladium*, even temperate *Bergenia*. This is from the "If it looks like an elephant ear then it's an elephant ear" school of plant names. But *Alocasia* have different needs than *Colocasia*; and a *Xanthosoma* is nothing like a *Caladium*. Even knowing only the genus of a plant can help you to grow it better as you begin to recognize patterns in the plant world.

Communication: The world is smaller than ever, and regional common names can have you talking in circles with the very breeders, growers, and collectors who might help you become better at what you love to do. Particularly with exotic plants.

Sourcing: A common name will not take you far when you are trying to get hold of something special. Even specific cultivar names can be used for more than one plant. To buy a Tesla Model Y, asking a dealer to see their electric cars will waste everybody's time.

The botanical name of a plant is made up of its genus and its species name, followed by a cultivar or variety name (e.g., *Xanthosoma aurea*) 'Lime Zinger'). With some hybrids where parentage

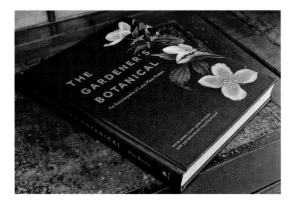

Finding an easy, accessible, and illustrated reference, such as *The Gardener's Botanical*, makes learning botanical names a pleasure.

is kept a secret for breeding purposes, or still being argued over by taxonomists, you may be given only the genus and cultivar names (e.g., *Alocasia* 'Architexture'). If the abbreviation "syn." is followed by a second name in parentheses, it's short for synonym and identifies the plant under a commonly used, but not officially recognized, name. Plant patents have made things more complicated, but that's enough to go on for now.

One of the easiest ways of increasing familiarity with botanical names is by labeling your plants. You will begin to painlessly associate the name with the plant as you see it each day.

As you use these names, continue to remind yourself (and sometimes others) that working with botanical names doesn't make you a snob. It makes you smart. Life should be a continual learning process—immerse yourself.

Tropical plants say "vacation" even when it's just another workday.

The Long-Term Commitment

Strong. Gorgeous. Versatile.

Who said that houseplants can never leave the house?

Over the last few years, houseplant enthusiasts have watched their niche hobby turn into a worldwide phenomenon. Through the magic of social media, apartment dwellers with hundreds of houseplants show us that you don't have to have land, a patio, or even a balcony to have a garden—you just need the desire to grow things, and the patience to manage an indoor jungle.

But what happens when apartment dwellers become homeowners? When window boxes become suburban lots and rural homesteads? Many of those plant parents will find that the plants that make them happy indoors make them even happier outdoors—and that giving those plants a summer vacation that involves a generous splash from the hose or abundant sunlight makes them healthier than they've been in some time. Some plants even flower or show intense variegation or color.

That's the Long-Term Commitment. It's a plant that looks great inside and out without too much work.

What Kind of Plant Makes a Good Long-Term Commitment?

You've probably been looking at many Long-Term Commitments in the tropical section of your garden center and thought of them either as tender summer garden plants or as houseplants. Time to think of some as both. The question is, which ones?

In general, Long-Term Commitments are plants that:

HAVE A PLEASING ARCHITECTURAL FORM

The point of a Long-Term Commitment is to provide both indoor and outdoor décor. When a plant has a great shape, it lends itself to this category. Whether it's the vertical lines of snake plant (*Sansevieria*) accenting a corner, an otherworldly air plant (*Tillandsia*) tucked in a basket, or the wild flourish of a *Monstera* against a stucco wall, plants create very different statements indoors and outdoors based upon their shape. Consider that when you commit.

ARE ADAPTABLE TO A LOWER LIGHT AND A LOWER HUMIDITY ENVIRONMENT

This is one of the more important characteristics to consider, as plants that require consistently high light and humidity levels will not look their best and complement your home if they are reaching for light (etiolating) or generally losing vigor in a dry environment.

HAVE STURDY LEAVES AND STEMS

Low light, low humidity, and low care. Winter with you is no picnic: it takes a survivor. In general, plants with sturdier stems and/or waxy leaves are the strongest candidates. Though these leaves are attractive to scale insects, the protective coating (or cuticle) on the leaves helps them keep more of their moisture to themselves over the winter. *Peperomia*, some species of *Ficus*, and *Hoya* are good examples.

CAN HANDLE A LITTLE ABUSE

Even though we mean to do our best, life happens. Therefore, the best Long-Term Commitments are plants that can handle the life that is currently happening to you. If you're just starting, you can't go wrong with a trailing *Philodendron* (*P. hederaceum*), a golden pothos (*Epipremnum aureum*), or the tough-to-kill spider plant (*Chlorophytum comosum*). All three pick up a lot of slack indoors and out—and look good doing it.

DO NOT SPREAD AGGRESSIVELY

Plants that recognize their boundaries are great Long-Term Commitments. Though they might spread and become bigger (*Peperomia*), they will not force you to break a ceramic pot to extract their roots and rhizomes (gingers!).

ARE NOT QUICKLY DISFIGURED BY PESTS OR DISEASE

. . . which is not to say that they are not affected by pests or disease. The large 5 gallon (19 L) umbrella tree (*Schefflera actinophylla*) that inhabits a bright corner of my living room will occasionally be bothered by scale by the end of the season. I treat it when I see it, but it is a large enough plant that it takes a full infestation to harm it.

TAKE A LONG TIME TO MATURE

The expense of a plant often reflects many seasons of growing, such as a large ponytail palm (*Beaucarnea*

The bright variegation on the leaves of this *Philodendron* 'Birkin' from the Trending Tropicals® collection makes it a stunning houseplant and a beautiful accent on a shady patio paired with other large-foliaged tropicals.

recurvata). If they are expensive and the preceding characteristics are met, it makes sense to commit to more than just a Summer Romance.

These considerations should affect not only your decisions at the end of the summer, but also your buying decisions at the beginning of spring. After all, doesn't it make sense to get the most out of your money?

Let's start by assuming you've got one or two houseplants that you've never brought outside. It's time to explore a whole new aspect of your relationship.

Summer Vacation

I love to think of reintroducing my Long-Term Commitments to outside conditions as a summer vacation, because I know that a growing season outside means that they are going to be healthier, happier, and at their very best when they come back in for the autumn. Much like us.

DON'T MOVE TOO FAST
First, give them a safe space.

Seriously.

Tillandsia can be placed almost anywhere—making a living floral arrangement out of just about anything.

A shaded outdoor holding area that receives morning sun and that is within reach of the hose is ideal, but as ideal conditions rarely arise in our lives, you'll probably need to create something.

In horticultural circles you would call this "hardening them off"—and even though a full-grown houseplant is not a seedling, it has adapted over several months to low light levels, no wind or weather of any kind, fairly stable day and night temperatures, and a dry indoor position. It needs time to readjust to outside conditions—just like you do. It may need to come back inside once or twice.

Even if your plant was in a sunny south-facing window indoors, it still needs this treatment to readjust to the powerful rays of the sun. I know that it's tempting to instantly deck that deck with amazing foliage, but if you do, it will only be amazing for a day. Wait.

REINTRODUCING YOUR PLANTS TO THE OUTDOOR JUNGLE
Day temperatures do not need to be summertime warm for your Long-Term Commitments to head outside, but they should not be cold. Aim for daytime temperatures in the high sixties (18–21°C), and nighttime temperatures no lower than 50°F (10°C). If you're still putting on a padded jacket to walk out to the garden, it's way too cold for your tropical plants.

Spring weather can be unpredictable. This is the time of year when, just like fall, you should be checking your daily forecast for an unexpected frost or freeze and scanning the ten-day forecast.

Cold frames or a greenhouse may also be used for this transition period, but with adequate shade cloth to make the transition a good one. Leaves will not only scorch quickly but will over-transpire in an initially hot environment. I prefer to wait until temperatures are warm enough, and then transition them outside to shady outdoor spaces, gradually giving them more light.

Gardeners are so busy at this time of year, waiting is easier than you think.

START THEIR SEASON WITH A NEW WARDROBE

This is the best time of the year to repot your Long-Term Commitments into fresh soil and fresh pots—particularly those that will stay in pots in the garden. Use a high-quality, well-draining mix.

Give the plant a pot that is a couple inches (5 cm) larger than its current pot and one with drainage holes if it is not a water-loving plant. I add a balanced organic fertilizer to gently coax them into active growth mode and ensure that new shoots are strong and supported.

If the plant is exceptionally crowded or root-bound, and its growth does not stem from a central crown, it may be time to divide it. Bromeliads (*Neoregelia*, *Alcantarea*, *Aechmea*, *Vriesea*, *etc.*) may also be ready to have their "pups" separated from the mother plant.

You can divide most plants by upending them gently on their sides and using a serrated knife or pruning saw, cutting between shoots where there are gaps—or in the case of the

A mixture of Long-Term Commitments and High-Maintenance Partners fresh from the house in late spring and sitting near the relative safety of a hose and a bit of shade.

bromeliads, as close to the mother plant as possible. Ensure there are roots on each division.

After any division or repotting, water the plant well and allow it to find its feet again in an area protected from sun and weather.

Finding Them Homes for the Growing Season

Because Long-Term Commitments are houseplants, they should be your first pick for the shadier spots of your porch, deck, balcony, or garden. Don't forget however that some of these tropical plants merely adapt to your indoor low-light conditions and would love to have a sunnier spot.

Sansevieria is one of those plants. I grow it in whiskey barrels in my shady patio, pots on my sunny deck and plunged into a lightly shaded bed in the middle of painted ferns (*Athyrium niponicum*). Most bromeliads, particularly spectacular *Neoregelia* species, need some sunlight to display the colors you fell in love with at the garden center, and which have faded after a winter indoors.

SHOULD YOU LOSE THE POT AND DIG HOLES?

This question comes up a lot when I'm talking to people about their Long-Term Commitments, and there isn't a straightforward answer, unless they are using them as single specimens on hard surfaces.

Ideally, you would repot a Long-Term Commitment in spring and use it in that pot all summer, allowing you to easily move the plant indoors when the season is ended, and resulting in less root trauma for the plant at that time. Holes can also be dug for the pot and the pot plunged, insulating the roots from environmental stress and nibbling creatures (see chapter 6).

In addition, plunging a plant in its pot allows versatility when designing. If you tire of something, or if something flags, you can easily exchange it for something else.

However, when root growth is restricted by the confines of a pot, plants are limited in their ability to seek resources during the hot summer season and must depend on you for everything. That means watering and feeding pots in garden beds that you might not otherwise feed or water.

It depends on what you want out of the plant and how much work you are willing to do. I use a combination of both methods. More than once I've hauled a large outside container inside at the end of the season because I didn't want to traumatize the stunning combination that filled it.

I regret those decisions two months later. Just sayin'.

Time to Bring Them In—What to Do and When to Do It

It's not the end of the season yet, but it's time to move some of your Long-Term Commitments inside—such as this *Schefflera* and *Strelitzia*.

By the end of the summer, many of your indoor/outdoor plants are looking their very best, having enjoyed elevated levels of warmth, light, humidity, and fertilizer over a long season. Even if you are not living in a region where rainfall is abundant, the chances are good that your potted "high-value" plants got most of the attention with the hose.

So here you are. Late sumptuous summer. The relentless drive of the growing season has eased and all you want to do is relax on that deck and invite a few friends over to enjoy the tropical effect you have created using a mixture of tender ferns, elephant ears, *Canna*, bird of paradise (*Strelitzia*), *Schefflera*, *Dracaena*, and turmeric (*Curcuma*).

Except that's precisely when you need to think about bringing some of them inside.

The longer you wait, the harder it will be on your plants—and eventually on you.

MAKING THE TRANSITION LESS PAINFUL

The function of a Long-Term Commitment (such as your *Schefflera*, *Dracaena*, or *Strelitzia*) differs from that of many of the other plants on your deck and in your garden. Whereas you might allow your Best Friends (such as the *Canna* and elephant ears) to go dormant as the weather

This healthy *Peperomia* came back inside early and is starting the season indoors with its bright variegated leaves intact.

gets increasingly colder, and bring them into your garage for storage, or where you may discard others altogether (such as the tropical ferns), your Long-Term Commitments will act as indoor décor during the long months of winter, and you want them looking their best.

That means giving them as little change in environment as you can and moving them inside before those indoor/outdoor differences become too great—particularly nighttime temperatures.

Though you may not notice any differences in your houseplant-to-be, and let the days get away from you, metabolic changes are happening within the plant to cope with those lower temperatures. When you finally and reluctantly let go of summer one night before the first frost threatens and haul the plant indoors to a drier, warmer, lower light position, it will most likely react by dropping a lot of leaves.

Not a great way to begin an indoor romance.

Pests don't just travel on plants. Before you take pots or ornaments inside, inspect them carefully. If this mealy bug gets indoors, you'll spend the rest of the winter fighting it.

For convenience's sake, this amalgamation of three whiskey barrels' worth of *Sansevieria* will turn into one large pot in my bedroom for the winter.

Instead, watch your outdoor nighttime temperatures. Before they are consistently in the mid-to-low fifties, do some "furniture rearranging" outside with your other plants, add a few fall fillers from your local garden center, and quietly remove and protect the Long-Term Commitments that will function as houseplants for the next few months indoors.

BATHE, INSPECT, AND TREAT

About two weeks before you've decided to bring in your plants, it's important to give them a physical.

I like to give the plant a hose bath to wash off dust and debris and thoroughly soak the growing medium. I

Treating plants outdoors means you don't have to worry about horticultural soap or oil getting on your furniture or floors.

then inspect each leaf and treat the plant for visible pests. Treating a plant under drought stress or in direct sunlight is never advised.

As well as benefiting the plant, this check-up allows you to re-evaluate whether you want to commit the time, space, and energy to maintaining that plant as a houseplant. This can change based on the overall health of the plant, life circumstances, and even summer furniture acquisitions, and you are wise to pay attention to the little feelings that tell you the relationship with that plant might finally be over. (See chapter 7.)

Hitchhiking pests such as aphids, spider mite, mealy bug, and scale can rapidly become a problem in a warm indoor environment without insect predators, as the population can go through several life cycles. Inspecting and treating the plant using an Integrated Pest Management (IPM) approach, and doing so again two weeks later, gives you the best chance of keeping pest populations low indoors.

INTEGRATED PEST MANAGEMENT (IPM)

Integrated Pest Management, or IPM, is an industry-utilized system of using the least-toxic solution first when combating pest populations.

I like to explain it by using a related analogy:

If you had a terrible ant infestation in your kitchen, you wouldn't treat it by tearing up your cabinets and removing your drywall. Instead, the minute you noticed it, you might try to keep the kitchen spotless, putting down some pet-friendly bait traps in out-of-the-way locations.

If those things didn't solve the problem, you might call an exterminator to professionally apply chemicals. If you still found ants in your sugar bowl, the exterminator would probably advise you that it's time to get out the keyhole saw and a flashlight and get ready to spend some serious money.

Chances are, however, that a quick reaction and an extra-clean kitchen sorted out the problem.

That's how IPM works. Using the least-toxic method first and following up with more comprehensive strategies as the situation calls for it.

When you're inspecting and treating plants coming indoors, this can usually be achieved using a mixture of manual removal, horticultural soap, and horticultural oil.

(See sidebar, page 46.) Horticultural soap is very effective on soft-bodied insects such as aphids, whereas horticultural oil works well on hard-bodied insects like scale by smothering them. Repeated treatments are necessary as there are several stages to a scale insect's life cycle, and eggs may be protected by the bodies of adult insects.

Horticultural oil is my go-to for most pests, but I start with horticultural soap to try and remove the majority of insects using my fingers. If the infestation is severe and the plant is of high value, after two treatments with horticultural oil over a two-week period, I will resort to spot treatment with the appropriate chemical matched to the insect and its stage of development.

THAT PERFECT PLACE

Once you've committed to another beautiful, oxygen-rich winter indoors, and bathed and treated your plant, you must decide where it's going. I would be ignoring human nature and the allure of lifestyle trends completely if I

didn't concede that this decision sometimes has more to do with the space you have, the look you want, and the windows you've been blessed with, rather than the needs of the plant.

Luckily, most Long-Term Commitments have a range of light levels and temperatures they can handle. Take time to research your plant and know both what it wants and what you can get away with. Sometimes you can get away with a lot, like putting a *Sansevieria* in a teenager's cool, dark bedroom, where it will receive a half a cup of water every four weeks and will look rougher than your teenager at the end of the winter. But sometimes, a poor position will kill it—such as giving a maiden hair fern just the right amount of light near an east-facing window . . . and directly over a heating vent. Know a plant's rules before you bend them.

For your larger, floor-bound or ceramic pot–housed plants, be kind to your back—and your floors. Use a furniture dolly and a helper to get them inside, and cheap furniture sliders to move them into place.

PLANT SAUCERS AND MURPHY'S LAW

In my shallow quest for form over function, I have ruined many a wooden surface over the years. We never think we have overwatered a plant until we come back and find it sitting on swollen, warped floors. Simply put, *it's always going to happen*—I don't care how careful you are. Therefore, invest in plastic saucers to go underneath the pretty saucers that you have.

And it's not just about drips either. Condensation can build up between the bottom of the saucer and the floor, and cause mildew and disfigurement of the surface. Small spacers placed between the surface and the saucer will keep airflow from allowing this to happen. It's certainly worth the effort on a particularly precious surface.

These *Sansevieria* have been pulled from whiskey barrels on a shady patio and placed in a corner of the loft for the winter. Light levels are low, but they'll be fine.

Indoor Care—It's a Long Winter

It's longer than you think when there are plants under your care. Long-Term Commitments need two main things from you during the winter months when sunlight is low and growth is slow: regular water and regular pest inspections. And once you get on a schedule for a beautiful, home-enhancing tropical plant, it's not much to ask.

When we neglect a plant and its appearance reflects that neglect, a curious thing happens in our psyche: The worse it looks, the less we feel like dealing with it. This never ends well.

Worst case: It dies. Best case: We end up with a plant that we can't wait to throw outside (probably too early) and that will struggle for the first half of the growing season to get healthy.

Don't build bad karma—give your plants what they need on a regular basis.

KEEPING THEM HYDRATED

Plants have different watering needs, even within genera. Some, like my large *Schefflera actinophylla*, can deal with water every week and a half and are totally happy. But my *Schefflera elegantissima* (false aralia) dries up, drops leaves, and generally sulks if it is not kept evenly moist.

Do a little research on your Long-Term Commitments to see if they like it on the dry side or on the moist side (usually on the plant tag), and use that information as *a guide only*. Your house differs from other houses, and some areas of your house are warmer than others, which will stimulate growth and subsequent water needs.

In general, plants are in their dormant season and do not need as much water as they do when they are growing outdoors. Watch your plants carefully and see how they are responding.

I wish I could say that I staged this photo. Sadly, I only grabbed my camera when the inevitable occurred. Always. Use. Saucers.

Organically Treating Your Houseplant Indoors

Limited space, soft furnishings, and carpeted floors means that treating your houseplants indoors can be a big deal. The trick is to not let problems get that big.

STEP 1 Pay attention to signs of infestation: On this *Schefflera*, sooty mold on the front of leaves has made me inspect the backside, only to find scale hiding against the veins.

STEP 2 If the plant is small, rejoice, and take it to the sink, where the treatment can continue. If large, pull it out completely from the wall or from furniture, so you can access all parts of it, and place large towels underneath it.

STEP 3 Remove heavily infested or yellowing leaves.

STEP 4 Though scale is best dealt with using horticultural oil, it is smelly and will create oily stains on furnishing and walls. I prefer to use horticultural soap indoors, and carefully monitor the plant over the next few weeks, treating again when necessary.

STEP 5 Mix horticultural soap according to manufacturer's directions in a good spray bottle.

Sooty mold on leaves is a sure sign that pests are feeding. Look closer and you'll see scale insects on this *Schefflera* leaf.

STEP 6 Use the wide, gentle spray pattern to thoroughly coat sections of the plant (I go stem to stem), covering stem and front and back side of leaf. Pay careful attention to the "crotches" between stem and leaf petiole.

STEP 7 Use your fingers (and nails) to remove visible insects, following up with a dry cloth.

STEP 8 If your plant is small enough and you can protect your surroundings from overspray, finish with a spray of horticultural oil, leaving the towels in place and making sure it is out of direct light.

Pulling out large plants and protecting your surfaces is essential when treating for pests.

STEP 9 If your plant is high value and continues to show infestation after a week, consider a systemic (nonorganic) granule applied to the soil after another soap treatment.

STEP 10 Don't let it get that bad again.

Thoroughly saturate both sides of the leaf, the petioles and stems, and use your fingers to help the soap do its work—wiping pests and soap off with a damp cloth afterward.

Plants that are overwatered will usually respond with yellowed lower leaves, browned tips, fungal growth at the soil line, and a distinct lack of vigor—their roots are in effect drowning.

Plants that are underwatered will usually respond with browned tips on leaves (yep, it's just to confuse us), wilting, and shedding of leaves. They simply can't support those transpiring leaves without adequate moisture coming up from the roots.

WATCHING FOR PESTS

No matter how hard we try, we will probably have one or two pest hitchhikers coming indoors with our plants and with their soil.

The best way to prevent big problems is to catch little problems, and the best way of doing that is to carefully observe your plant as you water it. A quick glance is not good enough. Touch the leaves—allow yourself to reconnect with this plant you walk by several times a day, and look for the signs that tell you it may be under attack:

- Sticky floors or shelves under the plant—or sticky leaves.

- Sickly appearance of plant—or a general feeling that it has lost vigor

- Yellowing of older leaves

- Stippling effect on plant leaves

- Spidery webs between leaf petioles and stems

- Black, wipeable sooty mold on leaves

- Visible appearance of pest—particularly on back of leaves

- Appearance of ants on the scene (that feed on insect secretions)

Treating a plant indoors is similar to treating them outdoors—with a few more towels. See sidebar, page 46. If you are lucky and have a warm day in the fifties, you can bring a plant outside to treat it, towel it off, and bring it back inside. Otherwise, be sure to protect your furnishings. You may think you'll be careful with the spray bottle, but just like with painting, you'll find splashes everywhere.

WHAT ABOUT FOOD?

Because my Long-Term Commitments go out every summer with fresh potting soil and fertilizer and are often fed with a water-soluble fertilizer during the growing season, I don't feed them during the winter months. First, they are not in a period of active growth. Second, feeding produces soft growth that is particularly vulnerable to opportunistic pests.

Feeding during the winter months should be done only if you are seeing problems that show nutrient deficiency, such as chlorosis (leaves yellowing with dark green veining). And then, only at half strength on moist soil.

WHAT ABOUT HUMIDITY?

While Long-Term Commitments will benefit from higher humidity levels in a house over the winter, it's tough to keep humidity levels high. This is one reason why plants with waxy leaves do so well as Long-Term Commitments. We'll deal with upping humidity levels for more nitpicky plants in chapter 4, The High-Maintenance Partner.

Too Much Required?

Long-Term Commitments are highly rewarding, but they still take care. If you're feeling the romance is dwindling, perhaps it's time to lean on your Best Friends for exotic garden accents. These ask very little of you over the winter, but they will give you so much during the summer season. Let's explore this relationship in the next chapter.

Asplenium nidus make excellent Long-Term Commitments, especially when a moisture wick is fitted into the soil. Its small plastic pot (with an absorbent cotton string hanging from the drainage holes) sits within the attractive, hole-free pot, on a ½-inch (1-cm) riser. This allows the string to dangle in a water reservoir and take up the moisture it needs. Guests only see a great-looking, healthy plant.

The Best Friend

Reliable. Easy. Valuable.

Over the years I have come to rely heavily on this group of tropical plants—which is precisely why I call them Best Friends.

These tropical plants are willing to go to sleep during our temperate winters. No light, no food, no regular watering, other than an occasional monthly check to ensure all is well. All they ask in return is a frost-free environment (35–45°F [2–7°C]), which you can offer with a cold basement, crawl space, or garage.

Just like our human best friends, there are few tropical plants that allow us so much leeway—yet give us so much reward.

In the fall, most of these plants die back to the storage organ of the plant, which can be a tuber, a rhizome, a corm, or a bulb—often just termed "bulbs" by industry professionals. These are dug from the soil or the pot is brought indoors. Many can be stored without soil to make storage simple, but some can be stored in the pots you grew them in, to make *autumn* simple.

Still others may be stored as dormant stems in pots, such as angel's trumpets (*Brugmansia*) or *Plumeria*, and will sprout again when temperatures climb.

Best Friends add so much in the way of color, architecture, and texture to your garden, and ask for so little in return, that they are a great place to start if you are just beginning to dabble in tropical plants. Just like any relationship, it doesn't have to last forever, but the chances are, you won't want to stop when you see what Best Friends can do for your garden.

> Best Friends ask for little but give so much.

What Kind of Plant Makes a Good Best Friend?

Fortunately, our Best Friends are also some of the most commonly available tropical plants in garden centers and are therefore the ones we are first likely to try. They are the elephant ears (*Colocasia*, *Xanthosoma*, *Alocasia*), the gingers (*Hedychium*, *Zingiber*, *Alpinia*), the colorful flowers of *Dahlia*, and the colorful foliage of rhizomatous begonias such as 'Escargot' and 'Positively Peridot'—all plants with storage organs that can be stored frost-free.

There are a few fibrous-rooted plants that I store this way as well (see chart on page 55), and no doubt a few others that you will find for yourself. If you loved a plant during the season and have easy space to store it in the dark, see if it will make it. That's how I found out rex begonia vine (*Cissus discolor*) could overwinter in a dormant state, as well as many of my (actual) rex begonias.

And if they don't make it?

Remember: Plants Die. It's Okay.

It's also a learning opportunity.

A mixture of some of my best friends—*Colocasia*, *Curcuma*, and *Canna* species in the rich, moist soil near the chicken coop.

Garage-wintered and potted up, *Canna* 'Red Stripe' await their seasonal home in late spring.

Bringing Them In

WHEN

Best Friends benefit from a hard frost that kills the foliage and prepares the plant for dormancy. This also allows our gardens to get the most out of them. When dealing with soft-stemmed plants, I find it easiest to cut them back to within a few inches of the stem and then dig. Plants with woodier stems can be trimmed to a desired height for storage, remembering that some dieback will still occur during the winter.

HOW
Digging

Most Best Friends are shallowly rooted. Loosening the soil around the clump with a fork or shovel and prying up the clump is usually all you need to do to get them out of the ground. When digging rhizomatous *Canna,* don't worry if a rhizome breaks during this process; but let it callus over for a day or two before storing. Be as careful as you can with gingers—they can be temperamental.

Never a better Best Friend—a white *Brugmansia* given to me as a tiny 5-inch (13 cm) cutting in spring has morphed into a work of art by late fall.

Rhizomatous tropical plants are extremely vigorous, and after a season they will push their boundaries. It's best to unpot this ginger, store it, and divide it next spring when it's in active growth.

Pots

If your plants are in pots and you're short on time, autumn just became a lot easier. You will need to trim any roots that might have worked through drainage holes and into the soil.

Many plants can be stored in their pots throughout the winter without issue, cutting back the top to make storage easier. However, soil will act as a "wick," rapidly moving moisture away from the storage organ or roots of the plant and into the air. Be aware that you may need to add a little water during a monthly check. If you are concerned about a high-value plant, take it out of its pot and use the towel-wrapped method outlined on page 56 to keep moisture levels relatively stable.

Once you've worked with Best Friends for a season or two, you'll get a better feel for what you can get away with.

Storage Methods

Storage methods vary depending on not only what type of storage organ the plant has, but also how picky it can be. For instance, though *Canna* and ginger species both have rhizomes (swollen stems that creep just below the ground), *Canna* will take far more in the way of abuse than gingers. You need to be a little more careful to get those ginger rhizomes through the winter—they like it on the warmer side of the range; and when they haven't had long enough to form a protective cuticle, they are very susceptible to rot.

Dahlia or *Oxalis* form tubers (an underground plant storage structure—think: potato). These are protected by a thick skin, but can shrivel if conditions become bone dry.

So, to limit confusion, I have grouped some of the most common Best Friends not in terms of their storage organs, but in terms of the method I use to store them in a dormant state: Bagged; Bagged with Sawdust; Towel-Wrapped and Bagged; and Kept in Pots (see chart on page 55). Some may be stored in more than one way.

Instructions for dealing with various Best Friends might seem complicated at first, but I promise that once you get into the swing of it, you won't be needing to check charts or planting depths or fertilizer ratios—you'll just do it. Like everything, it just takes a little practice.

Storage Groups for Some Popular Best Friends

Bagged	Bagged with Sawdust	Towel-Wrapped and Bagged	Kept In Pots
Canna* (large)	Dahlia	Colocasia* (small)	Brugmansia
Zonal geraniums	Ipomoea batatas	Xanthosoma	Colocasia* (large)
Tradescantia pallida	Oxalis (tender species)	Alocasia**	Cissus discolor
Lantana	Tuberous Begonia species	Hedychium	Dahlia
		Alpinia	Rhizomatous Begonia
		Zingiber	Plumeria
		Curcuma	Ruellia simplex
		Canna (small)*	Cymbopogon
		Manihot	Tibouchina
			Melianthus major

* Immature Colocasia plants benefit from being towel-wrapped, as do smaller, first-year-from-seed Canna.

** While Alocasia can survive the winter dormant, the plants tend to diminish over time. If you have space, consider treating them as High-Maintenance Partners indoors or in a cool garage with light.

BAGGED

After digging your clumps, lightly brush off excess soil and allow the bulbs/rhizomes to dry out for a day without direct sun. Then, put them in large plastic garbage bags, closing the drawstring of the bag very loosely, so a quarter-size hole remains for ventilation.

When labeling, use their cultivar name! I promise you will forget what they are in spring, and they won't offer to help in any way. Putting the bags in large plastic pots or trug buckets for storage is helpful. Trugs slide easier than awkward bags when you need to get to something in the basement.

Do not store rhizomes that show obvious signs of rot. If the rhizome is big enough, cut it back to fresh material and allow it to callus over for a few days before storing.

Though they are too heavy and awkward to act as Best Friends, bananas benefit from the same towel-wrapped method applied to easier plants. Here, an old comforter scrap has been peeled away from the bulbous base to find plump healthy roots ready for soil, water, and fertilizer.

BAGGED WITH SLIGHTLY MOISTENED SAWDUST

Generally, this method works best for tuberous species. If you have planted dahlias directly in garden soil, lift the tubers, lightly brush away soil, and store the clumps (attached to an inch or two of stem) in a plastic bag filled with *lightly* moistened sawdust—leaving the bag unsealed for ventilation. If they are already in pots, it may be easiest to store them in those pots on shelves after removing any roots that have left the drainage holes—but you will need to check on them to make sure they are not bone dry.

A note about moisture. *Don't overdo it*. I'm talking about a *hint* of moisture. Not wet. Not dry. Somewhere in between. If you leave the bag unsealed, it should create the perfect amount of humidity/ventilation to keep them plump for the season ahead.

TOWEL-WRAPPED AND BAGGED

Several years ago I approached the storage of my pickier Best Friends in much the same way I store fresh-washed produce in the refrigerator. I realized that, like a head of lettuce, they needed to be kept in a "sweet spot"—a place between wet rot and dry desiccation—and it was tough to achieve this by throwing them in a plastic bag or leaving them in a pot with dry soil that only became drier as the season went on.

When I wash and store produce, I allow it to drip dry, then I wrap it in a paper towel and put it in a recycled plastic bag for storage in my fridge. This quick storage hack can double or triple my storage time for vegetables. The paper towel both absorbs *and* releases extra moisture as needed. The produce stays hydrated but doesn't rot.

Applying an adaptation of this method using old towels when working with Best Friends such as *Colocasia*, *Xanthosoma*, *Alocasia*, gingers, and bananas dug from garden soil upped my winter survival rate to 95 to 100 percent. The towel also offers a certain amount of insulation against temperature fluctuations. Bananas (*Musa* and *Ensete*) are discussed in chapter 4 because their great size, weight, and need for vertical storage make them a High-Maintenance Partner in my book.

After cutting back the foliage to within an inch (2.5 cm) of the crown of the plant, I carefully wrap the moist (not wet!) recently dug root ball in a dry towel or rag, then put that in a plastic drawstring bag, gently closing the drawstrings. The bag is labeled and put in a pot to make storage stacking easier.

Though I can always take the easier way by throwing them straight into a bag as discussed above (and taking my chances), if I have a high-value plant, I'll make sure to store it with this little bit of humidity insurance. Towels are washed with detergent and bleach and reused next autumn.

KEPT IN POTS

Some Best Friends come in the garage or basement in pots and stay that way, especially the woodier-stemmed plants like *Brugmansia* or *Plumeria*. If I have to dig these plants from garden soil, I will knock off most of the soil and put them in fresh, damp potting soil in a plastic pot, cutting back the plant to retain some structure for next spring (there is still dieback of stems). *Dahlia* and *Ruellia* (Mexican petunia) can be cut down to within an inch (2.5 cm) of the soil line as they will sprout new herbaceous stems in spring.

The leaves of rhizomatous *Begonia* will dry up and fall off, but if the soil is not allowed to get too dry, the *Begonia* will remain plump while it sleeps.

Soil acts as a moisture wick between the plant's roots and the dry winter air—check on them once a month. If they need it, slowly add a little water so it doesn't immediately leak out of the pot. You do not want to water these pots like houseplants, as cold, wet soil will rot the roots. Err on the side of dry. It's a tricky line, but one you will learn to walk with experience.

Short-Term Storage Can Feel Like Long-Term

No matter how little your dormant Best Friends ask of you, chaos is just a step away if you don't take some time to prepare an area in your frost-free space for them. And, the more chaos you experience between autumn and the holiday season because you're tripping over bags of *Canna* rhizomes while you try to find the decorative pumpkins, the less you'll feel like doing it next year.

Instead, take some time at the end of the summer to think about how much you'll be digging and how it will be stored.

I like to use old A/V carts in my garage: they are usually extremely cheap at auctions and they have wheels so I can leave them against shelves dedicated to other household items and move them if I need to access those items.

Pots pulled straight into the garage are checked monthly to ensure the soil is not desiccated. Nearby, an old school rack holds zip-top bags of *Dahlia*s, *Ipomoea*, and smaller *Canna*.

Waking Up Your Best Friends

By the end of a long winter, I am more than ready to do some spring cleaning in my garage and usher those long-dormant plants outside. I usually feel the itch about three weeks before the beginning of spring as temperatures move from frigid to merely cold. As garage temperatures continue to adjust upward, some plants are beginning to sprout and stretch—unearthly white shoots emerging from black pots and garbage bags.

But with a last spring frost date two months away, there's still a long way to go before these plants will go into active vigorous growth, or indeed, be able to handle normal garden conditions.

MAKING A CHOICE

I can hurry them along by potting them up and putting them in a cold frame, or I can continue to (almost) ignore them.

I almost always choose the former option.

Leaving them means I will still need to monitor them in an increasingly warm garage and start to provide a little moisture to prevent them from exhausting their reserves. They will continue to stretch, which will weaken the plant overall. And, they'll probably be set back when these vulnerable shoots hit outdoor garden conditions. Overall, my display will be later and possibly a little weaker.

Whereas, if I pot them up with fresh soil and fertilizer, I can allow them to live in the dark garage for another two weeks until they emerge, having made healthy roots. After that they can go in a cold frame, where they will gradually acclimatize protected from frost and benefiting from warmer temperatures.

When my last frost date is behind me, those well-leafed and vigorous plants are ready to leave the cold frame and head to containers, beds, and plant swaps. Potting them up early means I can also pot up summer bulbs at the same time, getting a jump on their season and benefiting from the assembly-line aspect of the process.

Each year is different. I might pot up the majority of the plants but then leave a bag of *Canna* sitting in a dark corner due to time considerations. (Hey—spring is busy!) Other years they're all potted and "cooking" in the cold frame by the first day of spring. But that's the best thing about a Best Friend—they give us flexibility and understanding when we're not on our game!

It's early spring and I'm tired of reaching over plants for paper towels and detergent. Warmer garage temps have encouraged growth in the plants, and they are just as ready as I am.

A temporary cold frame can be constructed with CPVC pipes and plastic sheeting.

above In mid-spring, the difference between early potted-up *Canna* (foreground) and those that came straight out of a bag a month later is obvious.

left Three weeks later, the difference in vigor is still visible, and the *Canna* that waited will take a while to catch up.

above Newly potted-up tropicals go in a temporary cold frame outside once new growth begins to push up through the soil.

right Well-leafed, potted tropicals are now being protected from spring-browsing deer, not frost. They are happy to hang out for a little while, but really need forever homes soon.

top left Venting a mini-hoop house is easy. Simply clip back the plastic on one or both sides.

top right A waist-high working surface is essential to the process—here a potted *Canna* is turned out of its pot and will be cut into pieces to fill several pots.

left The temperature inside a glass-paned straw bale cold frame climbs quickly. Roll back the top side bales for ventilation. On very sunny warm days, remove the glass completely.

Potting Up Bagged Best Friends

If you've decided to get a jump on the season and move those Best Friends out to a cold frame, you'll need:

- An assortment of plastic pots in varying sizes—1 gallon (3.8 L) is a good standard size for many tropicals.

- Good quality potting soil. I prefer to use one with a wetting agent.

- Granular fertilizer, either synthetic or organic

- A sharp knife

- Sharpened pruners

- Plant labels

- Pencil or extra-fine permanent marker

- A large trug for organic waste

- A large trug for old towels

After unwrapping, bright, healthy stem and root buds stand out on this *Xanthosoma*.

BE GENTLE—WITH YOUR PLANT AND WITH YOURSELF

Begin by carefully unwrapping the plants you've worried about the most. For me—*Alocasia* and *Xanthosoma*. *Alocasia* take longer to wake up, so I'm just feeling the bulb for firmness. *Xanthosoma* tend to have a fresh, bright look to the base, with buds starting to raise, so it's clear if I've lost one.

If that's true and the plant has perished over the season, don't spend a second beating yourself up. We all lose plants over the winter. I expect losses of about 15 to 20 percent, but I usually do much better.

Instead, pay attention to what your dead plant is telling you. Is it dry and desiccated, or wet and rotten? Use that information to adapt your storage procedures next year. Treat every dead plant as a learning opportunity so it doesn't die in vain.

Unwrap the roots carefully and pay attention to what your awakening plant is telling you. This *Colocasia* has been allowed to put on too much growth, and without immediate attention would exhaust its resources and perish.

MAKING NEW PLANTS

Fill the bottom third of your pot with potting soil, and if the soil does not contain a slow-release fertilizer, add the amount recommended by the manufacturer (depending on the size of your pot) to the soil. For a gallon (3.8 L) pot, I usually use about 1 tablespoon (15 ml) of 10–10–10 synthetic fertilizer, but some prefer a higher nitrogen formula. Mix well.

After removing dead foliage, obviously dead roots, any rotten bits, and general gunk with a sharp knife, set the bulb or rhizome on top of the soil, spreading out any roots over the surface.

Generally, rhizomes should be planted with "eyes" up. Eyes are the parts of the rhizome that are swelling and beginning to sprout. Make sure there are a few visible eyes on each piece of rhizome you pot up. If you can't see any,

Elephant ears do not wake up at the same time. These three have been in pots for precisely the same amount of time. From left: *Colocasia, Xanthosoma, Alocasia.*

I always think I'll remember which is which, and I don't. Label your pots!

you may still plant it, but do so with other viable pieces so you are ensured leaves. I like to put 1 to 2 rhizomes in each 1-gallon (3.8 L) pot.

Fill the container with fresh potting soil about 2 to 3 inches (5 to 7.5 cm) above the bulb/rhizome. For *Alocasia*, I like to leave the throat of the egg-shaped bulb just above soil level. For gingers, I generally only cover with an inch (2.5 cm) of soil, adding 3 inches (7.5 cm) once they've sprouted. It can take almost a month of warmer temperatures for gingers to break their dormancy.

Label the container. When baby plants are emerging and you need to find homes for them but don't know what they are, you will regret not taking the time.

Knock the pot against the potting bench/ground to settle the soil. Top up if necessary.

Water the pots very lightly. You want to encourage those roots to search out water as they awaken—and find it. Do not saturate or they could rot. Once root growth begins in earnest, so does the watering.

Repotting Best Friends Kept in Pots

While you could conceivably add some fertilizer and roll those pots back into the garden (and I certainly have), it's much better for the plant to unpot it, inspect the roots, and plant it back into fresh, soft potting soil in a slightly larger pot, adding some slow-release fertilizer as recommended on page 62.

If a plant looks completely dead and dried up, don't lose heart. Pot it up, water it, and keep an eye on it for buds beginning to swell. Usually it just needs heat to get going.

TAKE ADVANTAGE OF THE DARK

If it is still quite cold outside at night and cold frames will have a harder time offering warmth, you can take advantage of your rapidly warming garage or a warm unused room in your house for a couple weeks until the plants emerge. No light is needed until then. If it is in your home, make sure you protect your floors.

BRING THEM TO A COLD FRAME OR GREENHOUSE

Obviously, timing is everything here. If you live in a very cold climate and start bringing out potted-up tropicals in mid-winter, they will freeze and rot. Try to time your potting up with your season, giving yourself two weeks before daytime outdoor temperatures are at least 50° to 60°F (10° to 16°C), and nighttime temperatures are usually above freezing. You will gain nothing from pushing this timing if heat is not building in your cold frames or greenhouse.

This is where you must watch your forecast and thermometers like a hawk. If low temperatures are forecast, use extra protection, or indeed, bring them indoors. I use old duvets draped over the cold frame in the late afternoon. You must also watch carefully for unseasonably warm days, which can fry vulnerable plants if the frame is not ventilated.

Bringing Them Straight to the Garden

Sometimes you just don't have time to deal with your Best Friends when spring is handing you rain and warmth and weeds and seedlings. You may find you can only get to them well after your frost date has passed.

You can buy yourself a little time by watering the bags and pots gently (so the plant does not exhaust its reserves as it begins to grow), then planting directly in garden beds or outside containers. You may lose a little spring bulk, but once the heat of summer kicks in, the plant will start to recover.

Give them the best start possible under the circumstances and plant them in rich, moisture-retentive soil, watering thoroughly and regularly. You will see a fair amount of sun scald as the new, light-starved leaves meet the sun for the first time. Cover them with shade cloth for a while to make this process less traumatic on the plant.

If you're doing this every year, consider if you may be digging too much in the autumn (see chapter 7).

The Best Friend You Can Completely Ignore

There are two further types of Best Friends: the tropical ones that are hardy in your climate and the temperate plants that only look tropical. Frankly, they both deserve books of their own.

Some tropical plants, such as *Musa basjoo*, the hardy banana, can survive, thickly mulched, when temperatures drop to -10°F (-23°C). These plants create an easy tropical feel, but will take time to get going, as soil temperatures rise more slowly than air temperatures. Experiment with a few "insurance divisions" of your subtropical plants. If your winters aren't too cold, you may never have to dig a *Canna* again!

If you're building a tropically themed garden, it's wise to work with a fair amount of what I call "Mocktrops"—plants that give you the look without the work—and accent them with plants that need overwintering indoors. We'll explore them in more detail in chapter 6.

Best Friends Forever

I can't believe I wrote that.

But at the same time, this sums up how I feel about this tremendous group of tropical plants. They're a gateway drug to the genre.

However, after a few years working with Best Friends and Long-Term Commitments, you might feel that you're ready to take on the challenge of a plant that needs a lot more from you than just a cold, dark room for five months. If that's the case, then you're ready for the High-Maintenance Partner.

Autumn has arrived, but this hardy banana looks fantastic. Once a hard freeze browns the leaves, I'll cut them back to the ground and cover the base with twelve inches (30 cm) of mulch. In lazy years I simply use the dead foliage.

The High-Maintenance Partner

Alluring. Irresistible. Challenging.

High-Maintenance Partners are high-impact, unusual plants that tempt us to venture outside our comfort zone to care for them outside of theirs.

Each time I buy an uncommon tropical plant that I've never tried before, I'm convinced I'll have it forever.

Straight from the garden center, the plant is at its very best. I cannot go back in time and see the grower fiddling with thermostats and irrigation systems, pulling snow off the greenhouses at two in the morning, or facing a mealy bug infestation that makes the heart sink. Nor can I see the truck that might have recently brought the fully mature plant up from a warmer growing zone because the grower had no desire to make her life more difficult than it already was.

All I see is a well-grown, pest-free beauty. The question is, do I have what it takes to get it through the winter for next season? Do I have the desire? Do you?

In that first growing season with a plant, the answer is predictably "yes!"

After a couple winters together, it may turn into a resounding "no!"

High-Maintenance Partners are usually high-impact, unusual plants that tempt us to venture outside our comfort zone to care for them outside of theirs. Unlike Long-Term Commitments they add little to the indoor landscape, and often provide more than their share of headaches. I consider it a victory when I have brought a High-Maintenance Partner (sometimes kicking and screaming) through the winter, ready to wow visitors for another long season outdoors.

High-Maintenance Partners test us and teach us. They not only help us to learn more about a specific plant or genus, but to learn more about our own limits, and set them.

Which Plants Qualify as High-Maintenance Partners?

For the average temperate gardener, tropical plants that meet several or all of the following guidelines may be considered High-Maintenance. They are plants that:

TAKE A LONG TIME TO MATURE/FRUIT/FLOWER

There's something incredibly satisfying in seeing a pineapple finally fruit. However, without the long growing seasons of our tropical cousins, temperate gardeners may need at least a couple years and consistent indoor conditions to attain the same results.

OFTEN NEED STRONG LIGHT

This may require additional (unattractive) light sources or shelving. Many palms that are commonly available in garden centers, such as kentia palm (*Howea forsteriana*) or lady palm (*Rhapis excelsa*), like more light than we can give them in an average house, and rapidly become spindly and plagued by spider mites if they don't get it.

REQUIRE CONSISTENTLY HIGH HUMIDITY

Keeping humidity levels high is difficult indoors but some plants absolutely require it, such as *Begonia luxurians*, one of my most challenging High-Maintenance Partners. Without a conservatory or greenhouse, we have to be creative . . . and attentive.

REQUIRE SPECIFIC WINTER TEMPERATURES

We tend to keep our houses at the temperature that suits us and our budgets, not our plants. It's tough to find the right spot for something that is temperamental, and even dormant storage temperatures count. *Caladium* bulbs are

You may find it impossible at the end of the season to say good-bye to an 'Escargot' begonia, and don't want to store it out of sight. You can make this Best Friend a High-Maintenance Partner, but you must figure out what it needs to stay healthy. Are you up to the challenge?

Combinations can pose problems. This stunning arrangement of Crown Jewel® Positively Peridot® begonia and *Neoregelia rubrovittata* 'Fuego' will continue to look amazing for a couple months. Then things will go downhill as the color fades from the neo and the *Begonia* aches for more humidity and loses leaves. It will spend the rest of the winter on life support in my office. But at least I got the chance to spend the holiday season with a rock star.

my picky child—they need constant storage temperatures of 60° to 65°F (16° to 18°C). In my cold garage with my Best Friends, *Caladium* bulbs turn to mush. Some years I make an effort, some years I have a Summer Romance with them instead.

ARE PLAGUED BY PESTS INDOORS DUE TO STRESSFUL CONDITIONS
It's almost as if the insects are waiting.

DO NOT HAVE A DORMANCY THAT ALLOWS BEST-FRIEND STORAGE METHODS
Some Best Friends can be 'pushed' to go into full dormancy in a cold garage even though they'd much rather keep their leaves and take a little rest from active growth in a cool bedroom—like *Alocasia*. But High-Maintenance Partners, such as woody-stemmed *Mandevilla*, simply refuse to die back to those stems unless it's permanently. Still others, such as tropical *Hibiscus*, will technically make it in the cold, dark garage, but will spend way too much time re-growing stems and foliage from the base.

ARE EXCEPTIONALLY MESSY OR UGLY INDOORS
Low humidity levels can create very ugly plants. Common tropical ferns such as Kimberley Queen and Boston (*Nephrolepis*), and *Asparagus*, are excellent examples, dropping a huge amount of yellowing leaves off of fronds and onto floors.

HAVE DELICATE FOLIAGE THAT DRIES OUT QUICKLY
Again, ferns are a great example. So are *Abutilon*, *Hibiscus*, *Begonia*, some species of *Ficus*, *Plectranthus*, shrimp plant (*Justicia*), papyrus, polka dot plant (*Hypoestes*) . . . well you get the picture. If the foliage does not have a protective, waxy cuticle, it is very susceptible to variations in moisture, light, temperature, and humidity.

ARE DIFFICULT TO DEAL WITH AT THE END OF THE GROWING SEASON

That can mean everything from spiny and dangerous to large and backbreaking. This is why my bananas qualify as High-Maintenance Partners. Though they go into dormancy using the towel-wrapped method (page 56), they are heavy and awkward, need to be standing straight upright to prevent deformation of the stems, and getting them back in the garden requires even more strength. Others might call them Best Friends, but I can't. (See sidebar, page 78). I still love them.

Most issues come down to the challenges of balancing and sustaining the correct levels of hydration, humidity, and light relative to temperature during a warm, relatively dry winter indoors. When these elements are not in balance, the plant suffers and you must also cope with the challenge of pests, which know when plants are stressed and attack them mercilessly.

Again, for average gardeners, High-Maintenance Partners are NOT Long-Term Commitments. We are not trying to enhance our living rooms with them and will not be tweeting out gorgeous images in January to other plant parents. A more achievable goal is to get them through the winter so we can enjoy what they bring to our summer gardens. And it might not be an attractive journey.

This variegated potato vine (*Solanum laxum*) has very thin, delicate leaves that cannot handle dry, warm conditions, and the terracotta pot is not helping. The leaves have completely wilted and may not come back from the woody stem.

The Perfect Equation

In very general terms, the following four "equations" should help you when trying to provide the right balance for the majority of your tropical plants, whether it's a High-Maintenance Partner inside or a Summer Romance outside:

Warm + Moist = Great

Cool + Dry = Good

Warm + Dry = Bad

Cool + Moist = Terrible

Warm + Moist conditions are active summer growing conditions. Warm temperatures, high relative humidity, consistent levels of moisture paired with adequate light. In a warm winter house, we can provide these on a micro level with glass enclosures, but on a larger scale without a closed conservatory, it's really tough.

Cool + Dry conditions are dormancy conditions. Cool (not freezing) temperatures, a naturally lower relative humidity (cool air holds less moisture than warm air), less frequent watering, and a source of light can bring the plant closer to a dormant state—or as a friend calls it, "stasis."

Warm + Dry conditions are what people, on average, naturally give their houseplants during the winter—sending pickier High-Maintenance Partners into a death spiral. The best Long-Term Commitments can weather this level of care for a season indoors, but they would secretly love a little more attention. High-Maintenance Partners drop leaves, their stems shrivel, and they are finished off by pests.

Cool + Moist conditions are perhaps the worst conditions you can give the majority of your winter refugees, as the plant is not actively growing, and disease and rot are encouraged. This happens if you are storing either Best Friends or High-Maintenance Partners in stasis in the basement, yet you continue to water pots and closed bags when they don't need it.

If you had your choice, would you rather stand outside during a summer rainstorm, or a winter rainstorm? One can be a lot of fun. The other opens the door to pneumonia.

Balance is the key. If you have conditions you can't change (like a warm living room), you must do your best to alter the other elements of humidity, light, and water if you wish to get your High-Maintenance Partners through the winter intact.

Consequently, we'll focus the rest of this chapter on creative methods of remediating those issues indoors and look at a few alternatives for winter storage that might make things easier on you.

Creating a Humid Environment

It's a fine balance between creating a higher relative humidity that your plants love (above 50 percent) and creating a serious moisture problem in a room of your home. If the room has not been built specifically for that purpose, and has very little ventilation, you have a lot more to lose than just an expensive plant.

Instead, I like to create micro-environments within rooms that balance the warmer indoor room conditions with the best humidity and light levels I can provide to match them. I can do that several ways.

A PORTABLE HUMIDIFIER

This isn't my favorite method as humidifiers quickly run out of water and, if kept in a small room with very cold outdoor temperatures, can create a moisture problem. However, humidity is not only good for our plants, but good for us. If you grow a lot of Long-Term Commitments and High-Maintenance Partners, and suffer from the effects of dry air yourself, it might make sense to run humidifiers in your home during the winter months.

If you heat with a wood stove or radiators, you can put a pan of water on top of them to save electricity and achieve similar ends. A cast-iron kettle with a small opening will work well on top of a wood stove, which is much hotter than a radiator.

GLASS ENCLOSURES

This is by far my favorite method of increasing humidity levels for High-Maintenance Partners with delicate leaves, though it often means cutting back my plant to fit underneath the structure.

Be careful with siting the glass structure so you do not inadvertently burn plants situated near south-facing windows and the raking winter sun.

WARDIAN CASE

This is a glass case with a wooden or metal base that looks like a mini greenhouse. Wardian cases were invented in the early nineteenth century by Dr. Nathaniel Ward. They quickly became invaluable for keeping newly discovered plants alive during long sea voyages. Winter is like a very long sea voyage. Wardian cases have the distinct advantage of being highly ornamental—instantly giving your living room a botanical flourish.

A Wardian case is both decorative and protective. Late in the season, these humidity-loving plants come inside before the first frost browns them.

Using Cuttings to Stay Connected

Some herbaceous tropical plants that might make your life difficult over the winter season can make your life a little less difficult if you take autumn tip cuttings and overwinter those instead of the "mother" plant.

Taking care of cuttings isn't "low maintenance," and they definitely won't enhance your interior unless you need street cred as a certified plant nerd; but they can keep you connected to plants you really wanted to grow next year and don't have room for. It makes a lot of sense for more herbaceous hybrid plants that would otherwise be considered Summer Romances and aren't started from seeds, or those you simply want more of.

Taking cuttings of *Tradescantia zebrina*

TROPICAL HERBACEOUS PLANTS THAT ROOT WELL FROM AUTUMN CUTTINGS INCLUDE THE FOLLOWING (BY GENUS):

- *Acalypha*
- *Alternanthera*
- *Angelonia*
- *Begonia* (leaf cutting)
- *Brugmansia*
- *Callisia*
- *Cuphea*

- *Dahlia*
- *Epipremnum*
- *Heliotrope*
- *Hypoestes*
- *Ipomoea*
- *Justicia*
- *Lantana*

- *Peperomia* (leaf cutting)
- *Philodendron*
- *Plectranthus*
- *Ruellia*
- *Setcreascea*
- *Strobilanthes*
- *Tradescantia*

Some of the above can be rooted using a glass and some water, but as they eventually need to be transitioned to a soil mix, I prefer to start there.

I root my cuttings using a Forsythe pot covered with a glass cloche or plastic bag. I have found that, for a home gardener, this method ensures the most success with the least work.

left When cuttings have formed strong roots and some top growth, it's time to replant. Use good-quality potting mix and a gentle organic fertilizer at half strength.

right A mixture of handmade and custom-made Forsythe pots sits on an east-facing windowsill, filled with cuttings taken in the early autumn.

A Forsythe pot is a terracotta pot without holes within a larger pot with holes and a saucer. A ring of perlite or vermiculite, or a half-and-half mix of both, surrounds the inner pot, which is always kept topped with water. The water seeps very slowly through the terracotta and into the growing media, keeping the cuttings evenly moist. A cover, in the form of a bag or glass cloche, is used to keep the humidity high.

Take 3- to 6-inch (7.5- to 15-cm) cuttings with a sharp knife or razor blade, cutting just below a leaf node. Try to avoid flowering shoots, but if it is impossible, remove all flowers or seed pods and all but one or two leaves.

Use a pencil or chopstick to make a hole in the growing medium and insert the cutting. Many of the above will take root without rooting hormone, but I find that a little #1 rooting hormone (there are three strengths) provides insurance and doesn't hurt the cutting. Dip the base of the cutting in the hormone, knock off the excess, then insert into the soil.

Cover the pot and keep the water topped up. Do not fertilize.

When the plant has formed roots, I remove the cover (slowly over time) and allow it to adjust to room conditions. Then the new plants can be transplanted into good potting soil. If you time this well, you may be able to transport the plants to cold frames within weeks of repotting.

Many shrub-like woody tropicals can also be started from cuttings (*Plumeria*, for example), but some may need a dip in a stronger strength rooting hormone to strike. If you're feeling adventurous, start with *Mandevilla*, *Coprosma*, *Codiaeum*, and *Hibiscus*.

NOTE: Propagating patented plants to sell or for any type of monetary gain is strictly prohibited by law.

Glass enclosures get cleaned in mid-summer in preparation for the autumn plant migration.

CLOCHE

Traditionally, a cloche is a glass dome that is inverted over a plant or plant pot. They are usually topped with a knob for easy handling and have become very popular as indoor ornaments in recent years. You can make a cloche using plastic jugs, Mason jars, cake stand covers, vases, or anything else that allows light in and traps moisture. Unless you are creating a closed environment for your plant (as you do in a terrarium or for cuttings), some ventilation is a good idea. You can achieve this by propping the edges of the cloche on small pieces of rubber eraser so the glass doesn't slip. Set the plant and cloche on a plate to protect surfaces from condensation if the cloche encloses the entire pot.

TERRARIUM

Generally, this is a closed system for plants where the nutrient, moisture, and light needs of a plant are provided in perpetuity through the natural cycles of transpiration, condensation, and decay. True terrariums do not have constant ventilation holes but can be opened for trimming and light maintenance of the plant. They can be Wardian cases or simple glass jars. Adapting one for a small High-Maintenance Partner (particularly a fern) can be an enjoyable learning experience and provides a great teaching tool for children.

HAND MISTER

A hand mister is a practical tool as long as you use it. It's easy to forget. I put a mister and the plants I need to mist in the kitchen and the office, where I spend a lot of time. If I see the mister, I use the mister.

PEBBLED TRAY

Setting the plant on a lipped plastic tray filled with pebbles and a constant supply of water is a very attractive way of providing humidity through constant evaporation, particularly if pretty or unusual pebbles or glass stones are used.

Invariably the tray will get mucked up with algae growth and can encourage mosquitos if they get in the house in the autumn. Make sure to clean it regularly. A solution of *Bacillus thuringiensis* (Bti) can be (invisibly and organically) added to the water if mosquitos are consistently a problem.

GROUPED PLANTS

Grouping plants with higher humidity needs together is always a good idea as they will provide some level of humidity for each other. It isn't much, but it's better than standing alone in a dry room.

Slowing Down or Speeding Up with Temperature

North Americans tend to keep our homes quite warm—far warmer than our temperate cousins in other areas of the world who know how to layer with sweaters and wisely keep the fuel costs down.

I cannot throw stones. In my house, the heat source is a wood furnace, which is safest burning hot. That means that evening bedtime temperatures can climb above 80°F (27°C) only to plunge to 55°F (13°C) in the early morning hours because we've cracked open windows to be able to sleep!

That daytime temperature says "grow" but other elements (light, moisture, and humidity) don't match up. Heat vents are everywhere—sometimes pumping warm, dry air near a plant's foliage and pulling the moisture right out of them.

If I've got High-Maintenance Partners, I've got a choice to make. And so might you.

If you are not creating a bright, humid environment for your High-Maintenance Partner that will allow them to cope indoors in a range of active growth temperatures (55–80°F [13° to 27°C]), or have quite a few plants that need pampering, it might be best to find a place where you can keep the temperature cool and provide some type of overhead light source just to maintain them.

A cool basement, spare room, or garage that *rarely* drops below 40°F (4°C) and stays in a 40° to 50°F (4° to 10°C) range will generally provide a decent green dormancy for many of our High-Maintenance Partners—or indeed Best Friends you'd rather remain in leaf, such as *Alocasia* and some gingers. It may trigger growth in one or two species if temperatures hit the higher end of the range.

Check the lowest recommended temperature for the specific plants you are growing. I have found that sometimes this is underestimated, and you can get away with the temperature being a little lower.

Keeping a room in a "stasis" range can be challenging. Try the following to make things easier:

- Turn off heat or adjust the vents to a finished room and crack a window slightly until the temperature is stabilized.

Ficus triangularis 'Variegata' is a fascinating, beautiful plant. But unlike *F. elastica*—an easy Long-Term Commitment—it requires very bright light. Without it, the plant will shed leaves and be attacked by pests. If you don't have a naturally bright place, you've got a High-Maintenance Partner on your hands.

- Utilize a dirt floor basement in older homes, where the temperature is often naturally in this range (or very close).

- Add a portable space heater fitted with a thermostat and safety features to your garage.

Over the years I have set apart a small room within my cold barn and set up a portable space heater with a tiny fan to move the warmed air around. For safety's sake, I only use oil-filled space heaters that act like mini-radiators, and I never place the heater within 3 feet (1 m) of any object.

If their pots have been plunged in the garden, it's easy to remove this princess flower (*Tibouchina heteromalla*) and parrot's beak (*Heliconia psittacorum* 'Choconiana') and keep them in a state of stasis in a 40° to 50°F (4° to 10°C) room with light. The *Tibouchina* will also overwinter fully dormant in a Best Friend state. (Mary Livingston Ripley Garden, Washington, DC)

Providing the Light They Need

Our sunny windowsills might provide decent sources of light, but they also subject plants to rapid temperature fluctuations. Hot during the day, coldest place in the house at night. Not good for a picky plant. It's usually best to give High-Maintenance Partners a bit of breathing room away from a cold window if you can.

If that leaves you with few options in a dim house, consider setting up small light stands in an out-of-the-way place, or positioning your High-Maintenance Partner under a lamp that remains on during the day. For those plants that cope just fine with low or ambient light (such as my beloved *Begonia luxurians*), your focus should be on balancing the humidity and moisture needs with the temperatures in your house.

For High-Maintenance Partners kept in cool dormancy, the good news is that light requirements are lessened as photosynthesis grinds almost to a halt.

An incandescent or fluorescent light fixture fitted with a grow bulb or full spectrum tubes that are comfortable enough to read by is often enough to keep plants ticking along. If you notice the plant stretching toward the light, add another fixture (and check that your temperatures are within dormancy range). Do not leave your plants in twenty-four hours of "daylight." Put the lights on a timer so they provide at least twelve hours, and sometimes a little more.

If you are using incandescent bulbs, remember that they give off a certain amount of heat and can burn foliage if the plant is too close to the bulb.

LED technology has made incredible advances in recent years. These lighting systems require a higher initial investment but use very little electricity and give off very little heat. If you're serious about keeping some of your High-Maintenance Partners in stasis throughout the winter, you might want to investigate LED options.

Tropical plants hang out in stasis in a cool, lit, and ventilated garage for the winter. Even the spiders find it appealing. (Prall Garden, Pittsburgh, Pennsylvania)

Best Friend or High-Maintenance Partner? Overwintering Bananas (*Musa* and *Ensete*)

Bananas in all their beautiful forms are one of the most exciting tropical accents in my temperate garden. I love it when non-gardeners visit from regions farther south and ask incredulously, "Is that a banana tree?"

Bananas tend to attract spider mites and aphids in a dry indoor environment, and those lush, beautiful leaves become shadows of their former selves. They are also very large plants, taking up a lot of living space.

Fortunately, bananas can be cut back to the growing point, dug, and stored using the Towel-Wrapped and Bagged method outlined in chapter 3, and are therefore Best Friends.

That is, until their second year, when they get heavy and awkward, their vertical storage requirements try my patience, and for stability's sake, they must be potted up a few weeks before they can go outside, adding even more heft to the package. In my world this moves them into a High-Maintenance relationship.

Yes, I can throw them away. But a four-year-old red Abyssinian banana in the middle of the border is something I get out of bed for in the morning, and I can't afford to re-buy them at that size.

Bananas are shallowly rooted. Once you've dug them, cut back the foliage, and cut the tip back to the growing point (where leaves are just emerging). You'll find they are often not quite as big as they appear.

A freshly unwrapped *Ensete* shows bright, plump roots that are looking for soil. Give them some.

These *Ensete* have been brought out of the garage and set against a shady north wall of the house to gradually become accustomed to outside conditions.

SO, HERE ARE A FEW HIGH-MAINTENANCE ADDENDUMS FOR BANANAS ONCE YOU'VE WRAPPED 'EM AND BAGGED 'EM:

- Bananas must be stored as vertically as possible. As temperatures increase, the plant will grow vertically—even in the dark—creating a deformed monster that takes a season to put right.

- Watch new basement growth for aphids—particularly during a warm winter season.

- When temperatures begin to tick upwards, the plant will begin to grow and rapidly exhaust its reserves. It's time to pot it up.

- Potting bananas up allows the plant to create new, fleshy, *stabilizing* roots that are invaluable when you finally put them in the garden. Though they can go outside straight from their bags, you will either have to stabilize them with stakes or keep righting them until they put out roots. That's traumatic for the plant.

- Once they are potted up and the temperatures are getting warmer, they need light and water. Put them under an incandescent grow bulb in the garage or a fluorescent shop light. This is only a temporary situation and need not be perfect.

- If the growing point is severely damaged during storage, *Musa* species may re-sprout with many stems very early in the season. This can pose a problem with dwarf *Musa* species, as your single stem becomes more of a low, clumping mound. Cut back to one stem if desired, allowing the plant to focus its growing energy.

Bring them outside when all chance of frost is past and set in a shady location with morning sun for a week so they can adapt to brighter outside light. Then, plant as desired.

Don't Forget the Water . . .

Let the previously mentioned "equations" guide you when it comes to watering your High-Maintenance Partners.

Warm + Moist = Great

Cold + Moist = Terrible

In the warm conditions of your house, you should be checking those plants twice a week. Though the plant is not growing at summer levels, it is still growing. Put your fingers down in the soil, which should be moist, not wet. A general rule of thumb is to allow the top inch of soil to dry out between waterings or you may drown your plant. Plants contained in a Wardian case or cloche will surprise you by how long the potting soil stays moist.

Plants in cool dormancy need far less water. My rule of thumb is to check them every two weeks or so and make sure they are not bone dry, adding just a little water when needed.

Can I Just Leave Them Outside . . . Protected, but Pampered?

That very much depends on the top hardiness range of your plant, your growing zone, and the lengths you are willing to go to. Some subtropical plants can be persuaded, others, not so much. Experiment and reach out to other "zone pushers" to find out what you can do.

Whether we're wrapping and mulching our plants outside, or pampering a few cuttings on the other side of the front door, when care becomes a major chore, we've got to ask ourselves a tough question.

Is It Over?

As I have continued to emphasize throughout these chapters, our limits are personal. I can think of several exceptionally talented plantspeople who think I have a high tolerance for pain when it comes to overwintering difficult tropicals. But, I can think of several exceptionally talented plantspeople who would look at me blankly and say—"Why on Earth would you grow that without a greenhouse?"

Just like the relationships with our human High-Maintenance Partners, the reason we keep going isn't straightforward. Most pros come with cons. Most points come with counterpoints.

In short, High-Maintenance Partners come with a price, and we pay it up until the moment we're done. Only you can decide when that is.

A later-than-average frost means this red Abyssinian banana can still contribute to the garden even as the landscape changes around it.

Friends with Benefits

Different. Daring. Delicious.

A delicious dimension to our relationship with tropical plants.

Let's have a little fun.

Until this point, we've focused on the exciting and sometimes unexpected accents that tropical plants bring to our temperate gardens. We've also learned how to choose them, grow them, and store them in temperate climates.

I'd like to add one last aspect to our relationship with some of these plants—a flavorful one. Friends with Benefits are tropical plants that heighten the excitement in our gardens, and heighten the flavors in our kitchens. Some are flavors we already enjoy, but don't realize we can grow, such as red hibiscus tea. Others, such as gingers, we've walked by in the garden center and wondered if that's the same ginger we pile on top of our sushi. The answer might just be yes—or "yes with a few adjustments."

It's a select group. In their native regions, tropical plants benefit from long growing seasons filled with heat, moisture, humidity, and often high topsoil fertility. Temperate gardeners working in cooler conditions are limited by the boundaries of two frost dates and cannot bring many of these edibles (particularly fruits) to maturity without a heated greenhouse or conservatory.

But there are still many plants from which we can harvest stem, leaf, root, or flower to create something a little different in our kitchens, and not all of them will need season extenders and heat mats to create something yummy. Apart from the most obvious use—flavoring—you'll find some make great teas, or can be sautéed as healthy greens, or can flavor and wrap your favorite type of fish for steaming.

To make the chapter easily digestible (that is the best choice of words here, I promise), I have picked out some of the plants you're likely to have the most success with.

Why Cook With Tropical Plants?

To explore! Creating and sharing interesting dishes and cool ingredients with friends and family is one of the great joys of my life—and getting my hands on fresh ingredients is one of the reasons I became a gardener (and a forager!). Thus, figuring out what I could and couldn't use from my tropical plants seemed like the logical extension of my cooking and gardening life.

Some of these ingredients we can buy in a grocery store if we are lucky to have one that carries them, but most of them are much better when harvested fresh. When you've made tamales with fresh banana leaves cut from your own plants, it is hard to buy them wrapped in plastic and Styrofoam and at least a week old.

DO I HAVE TO?

Of course not. The primary function of tropical plants, and of this book, is to use them ornamentally. This chapter, almost literally, is gravy.

You may not feel like making your green curry paste from scratch no matter how amazing it tastes, but what about adding some fresh lemongrass and makrut (kaffir) lime leaves to a pre-prepared mix, much like you might jazz up a canned spaghetti sauce with some fresh garlic and oregano?

You don't have to jump in headfirst. You can simply dip your toes in.

Early-season turmeric leaves waiting to go in the garden (*Curcuma longa*)

A weeding bonus! A handful of juvenile, edible shoots are harvested when weeding a vigorous stand of Mioga ginger (*Zingiber mioga*). I'll sliver these zesty shoots onto a salad.

'Candle Fire' okra is edible and a highly ornamental accent in a vegetable garden.

The sharp spines of *Solanum quitoense* protect the ripening orange fruit underneath those wicked leaves.

This hardy banana is a beautiful ornamental plant. When viewed through the eyes of the gardener-cook, it's also a valuable plant in the kitchen.

THE FINE PRINT

Before we begin, a few caveats. Many of which seem obvious, but all of which need to be said.

Not All Tropical Plants Are Edible

Some tropical plants are downright fatal, such as *Brugmansia* or *Ricinus*. Always make sure you are growing what you think you are growing. Never eat anything you are not 100 percent sure of.

Some Have Specific Edible Parts

Just as temperate gardeners wouldn't think of using the toxic leaves of rhubarb, and would carefully strip them from the edible stalks, some tropical plants only have certain parts that are edible. For instance, the small orange fruits of naranjilla make a tangy, refreshing juice, but you shouldn't eat the leaves or stems. (If the large orange thorns hadn't already made that clear.)

Some Need a Great Deal of Processing to Make Them Edible

With the notable exception of taro (discussed later), I have omitted these from this chapter. Cassava (*Manihot esculenta*) is one such edible. Without the proper processing needed to create a baking flour, and the starchy thickener, tapioca, cyanide will also be produced. Even if it did have a shorter growing season, there isn't much call for creating your own tapioca in your kitchen—thus it remains purely an ornamental in this book.

Not All Plants Within a Genus Are Necessarily Edible, or Good Edibles

Just because gingers aren't toxic, that doesn't mean you want to rip off leaves and start snacking. Try things that are meant to *enhance* your culinary experience, not just put notches in your "I tried that" belt.

Don't Gorge Yourself on Something You've Never Eaten Before

Your parents should have taught you this. Foods that we are not used to can make us uncomfortable. Try a small amount the first time.

Garden Centers Can, and Do, Mislabel Plants

Always double check the name of what you believe to be an edible plant with reliable, academic sources. If you have any doubts, *do not eat it*.

Dwarf variegated pandan (*Pandanus tectorius* 'Veitchii') is not the fragrant *Pandanus amaryllifolius* that flavors desserts and savory dishes. Don't ever make assumptions when choosing edibles—even within the same genus. (Pinkham Garden, Carrollton, Virginia)

Beautiful, Ornamental, and Edible

MALABAR SPINACH (*BASELLA RUBRA*)
WHAT TO USE: LEAVES, STEMS

An easy, visually sumptuous vine from Indonesia and India that thrives in the heat of summer when other greens are wilting, Malabar spinach leaves are deep green with contrasting red undersides and have red, twining stems—a truly beautiful plant. The succulent leaves may be eaten fresh or sautéed, and due to their mucilaginous texture, will thicken stews or soups. Violet and white flowers are produced on short spikes in leaf axils and are followed by deep purple berries that can be used as a food or fabric dye.

TARO (*COLOCASIA ESCULENTA*)
WHAT TO USE: BULBS (CORMS), LEAVES, STEMS

Taro corms are an important starch crop throughout Southeast Asia and Africa, and have been used by humans for millennia. The leaves and stems are also edible and used as a green or to wrap foods once processed by boiling or steaming. All parts of the plant must be cooked *thoroughly* before eating as they are very high in calcium oxalate crystals, which can cause terrible reactions if not neutralized in the cooking process. Peel taro roots before cooking and always use gloves to handle the peeled corms.

Taro and sweet potato tubers await the garden pot or the kitchen pot.

CILANTRO (*CORIANDRUM SATIVUM*)
WHAT TO USE: LEAVES, ROOTS, SEEDS

Scatter seeds in late fall and the delicate, lobed leaves of cilantro will give a fresh, lacy look to the spring garden and brighten almost anything from fish tacos to green curries. However, when summer's heat begins, and the plant rapidly bolts to flower and seed, the gardener-cook should look to the seeds and roots. The seeds are also known as coriander, and, pounded or used whole, are used extensively in Asian cooking. The roots are also highly edible and a little less pungent than regular cilantro—use them to flavor soups, stews, or curry pastes. In mid-summer, start more seeds for a cool-season harvest.

LEMONGRASS (*CYMBOPOGON CITRATUS*)
WHAT TO USE: STEMS

Lemongrass is an excellent flavoring agent for foods, giving them a lemony resonance that doesn't break down to just plain "sour" like citrus juices. It is usually harvested a few stems at a time once the stems have obtained some girth—later in the season for temperate gardeners. However, the leaves and immature stems can still be used by wrapping a few together and tying them up with their own leaves—creating a mini *bouquet garni* for your curries, stews, stir-fries, or sauces.

ROSELLE (*HIBISCUS SABDARIFFA*)
WHAT TO USE: FLOWERS, CALYX, LEAVES, STEMS

It is rare that an entire plant is not only beautiful, but fully edible—from flowers to leaves to stems. Roselle is one such plant—a hibiscus used extensively by many cultures for food dishes and mixology creations. In Burma, it is known as *chin baung ywet*, or sour leaf, and the leaves are used as a green and added to many foods. In the Caribbean, it is sorrel or *saril*, and the deep red flower calyces flavor drinks—they are naturally full of vitamin C. In the United States, roselle has been the main ingredient in the popular Celestial Seasonings® tea "Red Zinger®" since 1972. A must-have for vegetable gardens with a relatively long growing season.

above The vibrant red stems, green leaves, and delicate blooms of roselle (*Hibiscus sabdariffa*) make a gorgeous, edible accent in the garden. Photo credit: Ed Aldrich

left Slips of white-fleshed Cuban sweet potato emerge from a tuber immersed in water. These slips will be cut and planted as an inexpensive trailing (and edible) accent in containers.

SWEET POTATO VINE (*IPOMOEA BATATAS*)
WHAT TO USE: LEAF, TUBER

If it feels like you can't keep on top of your ornamental sweet potato vine, consider using the excess prunings to stir-fry or chop into stews. All parts of this versatile plant are edible, though in the pan, the lighter-colored leaves are more appealing than darker cultivars. If you planted in loose soil, you most likely will have sweet potatoes to dig up and hold onto for next year's crop. Store cold, and in the early spring, make slips for seasonal container plantings.

BANANAS (*MUSA* SPP., *ENSETE* SPP.)
WHAT TO USE: LEAVES, FRUIT

Temperate gardeners who wish to harvest banana fruit will need to wrap hardy species securely in the winter and pray, or bring tender species into a greenhouse, where they can continue their life cycle with little interruption. However, fruit is not the only thing that bananas give the gardener. Their large, flexible leaves have been used as food wrappers for centuries and are valuable to cooks in Southeast Asia and South and Central America for steaming or grilling all manner of savory and sweet dishes, as well as providing a plate or hand roll for serving. In Ethiopia, a fermented pulp is made from *Ensete* stems to provide sustenance during lean times. Blanche or steam leaves lightly before using them.

HARDY WATER LOTUS (*NELUMBO LUTEA*)
WHAT TO USE: TUBERS, FLOWERS, SEEDS, STEMS

Another fully edible, gorgeous plant—this one for the water—tropical water lotus are used throughout the tropics. Their fascinating tubers are eaten pickled or cooked. Their seeds can be cooked or popped. Their delicate flowers can be used in soups, and their young leaves and stems are cooked as a green. Unfortunately, the tropical species *Nelumbo nucifera* is not hardy for temperate gardeners and will cost you a fortune to prepare for the table. Enter *N. lutea*, a North American native, which retains all the exotic charms and usefulness of its tropical cousin, but is hardy to -10°F (-23°C). Yes, it's a bit of a cheat. But it's a beautiful, useful cheat. And it grows fast.

OCA (*OXALIS TUBEROSA*)
WHAT TO USE: TUBERS

Given soft, fairly fertile soil, oca acts as a weed suppressor at the base of other ornamentals and will soften hard edges in your landscape with its shamrock foliage and red stems. Late in the season, small, waxy tubers form in the soil and are about the size of fingerling potatoes. The plant is prolific and just a few seed tubers can yield several pounds worth of produce in a multitude of colors depending on the cultivar. Use caution when preparing, as oca is high in oxalate, which can be irritating to skin and mucous membranes. Letting them dry in the sun for a week after rinsing several times is recommended. Oca can be eaten raw when prepared correctly but is most often boiled and steamed much like a potato.

It's autumn. But as the potted tender plants come in and find space in the kitchen, there are still a few weeks left that I can harvest banana leaves.

Naranjilla fruits ripen among sharp spines.

NARANJILLA (*SOLANUM QUITOENSE*)
WHAT TO USE: FRUIT

Naranjilla (also known as lulo) is an otherworldly, unusual plant used extensively in South and Central America. It's large-lobed hairy leaves sport orange-tipped thorns along their purple ribs and along the stems. In the late season, attractive orange fruits with green pulp will ripen. Mash the peeled fruit with sugar and mix with fresh lime juice and water to create a refreshing drink called *lulada*; or make popsicles using evaporated milk, naranjilla juice, sugar, and mashed, peeled fruit. The leaves and stems of naranjilla are not edible. Naranjilla is extremely susceptible to frost, like most members of the Solanaceae family, such as tomatoes and potatoes.

JAPANESE GINGER (*ZINGIBER MIOGA*)
WHAT TO USE: FLOWER BUDS, FLOWERS, YOUNG SHOOTS

One of the hardiest gingers you can grow, Japanese ginger comes in plain and variegated leaf patterns and is more vigorous in a temperate shade garden than its cousins, emerging in late spring to 4 to 5 feet (1.2 to 1.5 m) tall. The young shoots can be harvested and cooked (old shoots are said to be toxic), but it is the late-season unopened flower buds that are considered a delicacy in Japan—pickled, fried as tempura, or shredded fresh as a garnish with a tangy, ginger/onion taste. Flowers form at the base of the plant, right at the soil line, so keep your eyes peeled!

Held right at the soil line, the flowers of Japanese ginger are lovely, and edible, but it's really the flower buds you're looking for.

COMMON GINGER (*ZINGIBER OFFICINALE*)
WHAT TO USE: RHIZOMES, STEMS

It takes ten to twelve months to mature the thick-skinned ginger rhizomes you see at the grocery store, but only eight or nine months to grow young ginger, which is the thin-skinned, tender rhizome harvested in late fall and pickled to create the sushi garnish, *gari*. Young ginger is very difficult to obtain and makes it worth growing if you love sushi as much as I do. The attractive young shoots and leaves can also be chopped and used as a garnish. Get this crop started as early as possible for best results. Sprout "seed" rhizomes on a warm countertop for about a week, then cover with an inch (2.5 cm) of good soil and keep at room temperature until shoots are 2 inches (5 cm). Plant in deeper pots and keep warm and lit, planting outside after the last frost.

Plump ginger rhizomes flavor refreshing ginger beer.

Turmeric rhizomes are unwrapped after a long winter season. This large clump originally grew from two finger-sized rhizomes planted the previous spring.

TURMERIC (*CURCUMA LONGA*)
WHAT TO USE: ROOTS, LEAVES, FLOWERS

The finger-sized rhizomes of turmeric are making quite a name for themselves these days, and feature in everything from tea to curry to healing supplements; but they are also a beautiful tropical plant—somewhat late to emerge, but vigorous once started. The wide green leaves of *C. longa* are shaped like broad swords and the flowers/bracts like colorful pinecones, appearing on the plant in late fall. Grow like ginger (on page 91) and harvest the orange fingers from the outer perimeter of the plant or use flowers as a garnish. Leaves can wrap food. Rhizomes can be grated or pounded into many dishes. Turmerics are hardier than most gingers and several can survive mulched in the garden to 5°F (-15°C).

GALANGAL (*ALPINIA GALANGA*)
WHAT TO USE: RHIZOMES

Galangal is that mystery flavoring ingredient in Southeast Asian foods that takes them from good to great. It is larger, more fibrous, and more pungent than common ginger, but grows similarly into a fine foliage plant in full sun. Like ginger and turmeric, it must be started very early indoors or in a warm greenhouse. When the frost kills the leaves, bring in for fresh dishes and freeze the rest. It's usually best to start with new starts next year as galangal does not have a protective skin to get it through winter and can be tricky. Ginger, turmeric, and galangal tubers can be kept frozen and grated as needed into dishes using a fine grater. Use waxed paper to easily catch the gratings or grate directly over the pot.

PANDAN (*PANDANUS AMARYLLIFOLIUS*)
WHAT TO USE: LEAVES, ROOTS

A Long-Term Commitment you can steal from, pandan is a sought-after flavoring agent in Southeast Asian cooking and an attractive plant whose leaves resemble that of a wide, spiky *Dracaena*. Unlike *Dracaena* however, those leaves are highly fragrant and add a grassy, vanilla-almond note to rice, chicken, and dessert dishes. They are also used medicinally in many cultures as a sedative and a traditional treatment for diabetes. In the garden, pandan prefers dappled light and will very slowly grow into a small tree. Indoors, give it bright, indirect light, and experiment with its unique flavor as the days draw in.

ACHIRA (*CANNA INDICA*)
WHAT TO USE: LEAVES, RHIZOMES, FLOWERS

Canna grows so vigorously and multiplies so rapidly that at the end of the season you may be overrun with rhizomes. If you are growing the fairly hardy species *Canna indica* (syn. *C. edulis*), also known as achira or Indian shot, you might want to take some of those extra rhizomes indoors for the table, as they are used as a starchy staple in many South American cultures. Larger and rounder than other species, they can be roasted or boiled and mashed, though they do tend to be fibrous. The red or yellow blossoms are also edible, and petals can be used raw to garnish salads and other dishes. Leaves can be used to serve or wrap dishes. *Please do not mistake calla lilies for canna lilies. Calla (Zantedeschia) are toxic*—another reason I prefer to use botanical names.

Canna indica vertically accenting the soft textures of *Miscanthus sinensis* 'Gracillimus'

Grow a Green Curry Bed!

Green curry is one of the most popular curries in Thai cooking, and fresh ingredients such as pungent gingers, fragrant lemongrass, Thai basil, tiny eggplants, hot chilis, crispy beans, and zesty coriander can really make yours stand out. Why not have a little fun growing most of the ingredients in one raised bed, much like a Pizza or Spaghetti Bed? If you make green curry as much as I do, you'll appreciate not having to run out to the store for some of those vegetables.

My curry bed focuses on hard-to-find ingredients for a sumptuous green curry, such as 'Kermit' Thai eggplant.

You'll have the best chance of success if you start galangal, turmeric, and ginger indoors very early in the season, as well as seeds of the specific varieties of eggplant and pepper you want. Garden centers very rarely carry the tiny round eggplants so popular in Thai cookery such as 'Kermit.'

Consider plunging a pot of makrut (or kaffir) lime in your curry bed to keep all your ingredients handy (*Citrus hystrix*). In autumn you can bring this High-Maintenance Partner inside.

Enrich your bed liberally with well-rotted manure and plant it after all chance of frost is gone. Or construct a temporary hoop house over the bed to boost heat a few weeks early, giving the lemongrass a northeast corner of the bed so it doesn't shade the rest of the plants. Pole beans can be grown vertically on a teepee structure made from bamboo lashed together once your frost date has passed.

Ensure that your bed is kept well watered and, if necessary, prune your plants to ensure they play well together. Harvest as vegetables mature, taking small divisions from the outer perimeter of the gingers later in the season. When the cilantro goes to seed, collect the seed, harvest the roots, and don't forget to sow more for the fall season.

Planting up a curry bed in late spring

The curry bed in high summer

Preparing curry bed produce for a fresh, delicious green curry in mid-summer

Grocery Store as a Plant Nursery?

A fun way to break into tropical plants cheaply in early spring is to visit your local world market or grocery store that specializes in flavors and ingredients from many regions.

Here you'll find exotic sweet potatoes, basic taro, ginger, galangal, and turmeric that you can use to sprout new plants and add a little tropical to your existing garden.

As with most vegetables shipped for storage, tubers and rhizomes are cleaned and sometimes treated to prevent sprouting, so you must examine your potential plant carefully. Healthy, firm rhizomes or tubers are what you are looking for. Do not choose anything that is withered or dried or exhibits signs of mold.

If you scan carefully, you may just find the greenish-white nodes of gingers beginning to rise slightly. Bring firm rhizomes home and allow them to rest on the countertop for a couple days in indirect light. If they begin to wither, discard them. When nodes start to swell, it's time to cover with a couple inches of soil and let stems grow 2 inches (5 cm) before potting them in a bigger pot. Keep them warm and watered.

Make "slips" from your sweet potatoes by inserting four toothpicks into the sides of the tuber and placing in a glass of water, with three-quarters of the tuber submerged. Soon, the tuber will send out several shoots with roots—cut those free of the tuber with a sharp knife and plant for a decorative (and edible) tropical vine.

You'll find that the foliage grown from these grocery store plants is often just as vigorous as that of the special plants you have carefully sourced—but that means that you needn't worry about keeping them protected over the winter. Use these cheap accents as Summer Romances for the season and simply put a few on your grocery list at the end of the winter—indulging in a tropical plant dalliance without paying the full nursery price.

A mix of grocery store taros, turmeric, and sweet potatoes in the foreground weave together with "real" ornamentals: Coleus 'Main Street Beale Street,' popcorn plant (*Senna*), and 'Desana Lime' sweet potato vine.

Take your tablescape up a notch with a tropical theme.

Fun with Tropical Tablescapes

Don't forget to use your tropical plants in your tablescapes—particularly if you are making an exotic meal or serving a convenient takeout! Here are just a few ideas:

- Banana and *Canna* leaves make gorgeous placemats.

- Wrap napkins with lemongrass foliage tied in a knot.

- Forget about vases full of flowers and use three to five striking leaves arranged simply in a glass vase.

- Overlap banana leaves down the center of the table as a living runner.

- Use washed banana, *Canna,* or ginger leaves to line serving platters.

- Place air plants (*Tillandsia*) in small terracotta pots and run them down the center of the table alternating with votives.

- If you only have a few air plants, showcase them in a centerpiece of interesting twigs.

- Papaya seeds scooped from ripe fruits, dried, and put in a gauze bag with instructions for next year's garden make a great party or plate favor. If your guests see the tree in your garden, they'll be thrilled to have some seed!

Stumped for Ideas?

You can find the recipes for these tempting tropical dishes at smalltowngardener.com/recipes.

Steamed and ready for the plate, Chicken Chipotle Tamales utilize one of the gardener-cook's most useful tropical tools: banana leaves.

Tri-colored Taro and Sweet Potato Chips are just as tasty as they are beautiful.

Jamee's Frozen Hibiscus Gimlet is both refreshing and stunning. Serve this cocktail in late summer, when guests can wander the garden and see the plants involved in its creation.

Tantalizing Mioga Tempura is a special meal to have with a special group of friends.

THE
DESIGN

Gardening with Tropical Plants

Atmosphere. Abundance. Attitude.

Utilize tropical plants deliberately, aware of the statement you're making.

There is no doubt that tropical plants up your garden's game.

They are unusual, and people notice them. They are lush and create a vacation atmosphere in everyday life. They are fast-growing, and can bring energy, architecture, and awe to a young garden very quickly.

However, due to these same factors, they can also stick out awkwardly, alter the flavor of our gardens, and become a crutch upon which we disproportionately depend.

Don't let that stop you plunging in! Instead, use the inherent drama of tropical plants *deliberately*, aware of the statement you are making as a gardener in a temperate climate—because you're definitely making a statement.

Let's explore the different ways we can use tropical plants—in containers, in water features, and in the garden itself, starting with the way most gardeners become acquainted with tropicals—as container plants.

Tillandsia can help you expand your definition of "container."

Containers

Using containers is the best way to experiment with tropical plants. Many of the same design and growing principles apply to using tropicals in the garden generally, so when you break out of containers, you'll be a step ahead. It's a great way to have a little fling.

Why?

- Unusual leaf textures and colors provide strong (and easy) contrast to traditional plants.

- Tropical accents carry containers through the hot summer season with style.

- A tropical oasis can be created on a small patio or balcony with only a few plants.

- Colorful ceramic or plastic containers can complement the tropical theme.

- Some tropicals take well to small container water features.

- Soil, water, and fertilizer needs can be tailored to plants in a container.

- Containers warm up faster than garden soil for those in cooler climates.

- Container culture is well suited to Long-Term Commitment choices, which can be moved inside to decorate indoor spaces once the season ends.

Containers allow gardeners to easily experiment with shapes, textures, and colors. (Garden of Peggy Bier, Tysons Corner, Virginia)

Canna Tropicanna®
and red bananas
will grow large
over the season,
but this container
is big enough
to handle them.
(Brookside Gardens,
Wheaton, Maryland)

WHEN CHOOSING A TROPICAL PLANT FOR YOUR CONTAINERS, CONSIDER:
Size

Using tropical plants that work in proportion to one another and to their container is *critical* when creating what is in effect a micro-garden. How many containers have you seen with a "thriller" three or four times taller than the plants that surround it? How much did your palm itch to grab a pair of pruners and cut it in half?

This is particularly true for containers that utilize *Canna*—for a long time one of the more available tropical foliage plants in garden centers. Some cultivars can grow up to 10 feet (3 m) tall, and will not only dwarf their companions, but look ridiculous in a small pot. Thankfully, there are dwarf options when it comes to container focal points such as *Canna*, bananas, and elephant ears.

Conversely, few plants can beat tropicals when it comes to creating scale on a large level. An *Ensete* or *Canna* in a showstopping container can frame an entrance and completely reframe a garden, giving you almost instant structure in a temporary seasonal display.

Neoregelia rubrovittata 'Fuego' and *Begonia* 'Positively Peridot®' make well-behaved summer companions.

This *Alcantarea* needs delicate companions such as this brake fern (*Pteris cretica*) and a Bonfire® Begonia that takes well to pinching. (Chanticleer Garden, Wayne, Pennsylvania)

Vigor

Just as a too-tall vertical accent can create awkward proportions in a small container, highly vigorous selections can overcome their companions in a shared growing space. Choose either slower-growing plants or those that can be surreptitiously pruned without damaging their appearance or health. Match the vigor of your tropical plants carefully.

For instance, a *Neoregelia* bromeliad is unlikely to take over your pot during the summer, and looks great matched with large-leafed begonias, but a giant bromeliad like *Alcantarea imperialis* 'Malbec' will provide little breathing room. That's great if you underplanted with a trailing begonia, but if you didn't, "pruning" the *Alcantarea* by cutting the growing point in half will not work out for anyone.

The strong foliage colors in *Alpinia zerumbet* 'Variegata' need a careful hand to pair them. Here, BIG® *Begonia* provide a gentle green leaf contrast with pink blossom accents.

Shade or Sun Lover

Many tropical plants are very happy in shady or partially shady conditions and grow with the vigor of their temperate cousins located in sunnier locations. This means that your patio, your covered front porch, or shady steps can still look just as lush as your sunny areas.

For a healthy and vigorous season, make sure you're matching up sun lovers and shade lovers just as you would with traditional combinations—and matching those combinations to your site.

Foliage Color

Tropical plants are often high-contrast plants. It's much of the reason why we love them. But sometimes that look can go from "Wow!" to "What?!?" when large foliage plants are matched badly. If your focal point is making a strong, multicolored statement, such as *Cordyline fruticosa* 'Harlequin,' consider adding some plainer foliage that picks up just one of those colors, such as *Dracaena deremensis* 'Limelight'—enhancing, not competing with, its companion.

Do you adore a special, stunning container, but don't want to add to the daily watering chores? Pots don't necessarily need to contain plants to create exquisite combinations in the garden. (Chanticleer Garden, Wayne, Pennsylvania)

Some foliage plants, such as this cluster of bromeliads (*Aechmea fasciata*) are not only stunning in leaf, but also in their long-lasting flowers. Others not so much. Consider all aspects of the tropicals you plant, and whether you can expect flowers in your growing season.

Flower Color

I have to confess to a strong preference for foliage over flower, and sometimes I am still surprised when my tropical foliage plants suddenly flower in the middle of the season. If I haven't thought about the color of the flower when planting, it can make for some jarring results. Particularly in a container.

Know what you're planting—foliage AND flower—and have a sharp pair of pruners convenient if you want to keep it all about the foliage.

Water Needs

Tropical plants are heavy drinkers. Using them in containers means they are completely dependent upon you, as containers dry out more quickly than plants in beds. Using glazed ceramic or plastic containers (particularly self-watering containers) can alleviate this issue, as can using high-quality potting soil.

Always consider where your nearest source of water is when siting your containers. It should be the first thing you think about, because I assure you it will be the only thing you're thinking about four months later.

For those in dry climates who long for a bit of lush, using containers allows the gardener to experiment with tropical plants without wasting precious water with sprinklers. Container drip irrigation or self-watering containers are a great way to go—again, think strategically when siting..

Water Gardens

Some tropical plants appreciate a wet environment, particularly *Colocasia*, *Canna*, and papyrus; and of course, tropical lotus and water lilies, water lettuce (*Pistia stratiotes*), and water hyacinth (*Eichhornia crassipes*).

You can use the large leaves of *Colocasia* at different levels (inside and outside the pond) to hide the unattractive sides of a preformed pond; or create strong vertical lines with papyrus (especially the giant *Cyperus papyrus*); or add color to your pond with the variegated foliage and flamboyant flowers of *Canna*. Tropical plants add a lush, Amazonian feel to the entire water feature, so if your desire is to heighten a more traditional, temperate scene, use only one or two as striking accents. They grow quickly.

Colocasia, *Canna*, and papyrus species are happiest in the boggy margins or only just submerged. For best results, allow the surface of the soil to be very near the top of the water, using bricks to achieve that height. Not all *Canna* and *Colocasia* species adore a nonstop summer swim, so if you are seeing a lack of vigor in your plant, adjust the height or remove it altogether. Again, experiment.

For potted plants, put a large rock in the base of the pot you are submerging and cover the soil with pea gravel to stop it floating away. I have found that fabric pots work extremely well as they can be squeezed to fit into tight corners and the edges rolled down to accommodate the water level.

When using fertilizer, use slow-release tablets (shaped into pill format) to insert into the soil of the pot so it does not immediately end up in the water.

Water lettuces and water hyacinth mingle and bloom with papyrus in a containerized water feature.

Submerge plants such as *Canna* and *Colocasia* only at soil level, having secured the soil with gravel.

After a winter's dormancy, tropicals can look a little sad early in the season, which is why it's so important to grow a balanced mix of temperate and tropical plant choices if you wish to maintain a three- or four-season garden.

Except for true water plants, the tropicals you use in your designs can be brought in and stored as you would store the species if you hadn't had them in a bath all season. Trim the pots of excess roots, and allow them to dry considerably if storing in a cold situation.

One of the simplest ways I use tropical plants is to throw a water lettuce and water hyacinth in a large, wide decorative bowl in the middle of the table on my deck in late spring. Within three weeks, I have multiple plants filling the bowl, I've added a Mosquito Dunks® to combat the blood-suckers, and I've got a gorgeous centerpiece that attracts frogs and dragonflies.

That's a water feature, though you won't necessarily find it in books on ponds. Both of these plants are highly invasive in warm tropical climates and can choke out native vegetation in waterways; but in a bowl on my deck in a cold-winter climate, they are safe. I can enjoy them as a Summer Romance, and let them die when the cold winds blow.

A tropical castor bean energizes a temperate juniper, creating a combination that is more than the sum of its parts.

Red Abyssinian bananas provide height along the author's garden path, cleverly concealing the now mildewed foliage of a late spring lilac.

Bold? Or garish? Though beauty is in the eye of the beholder, the success of a tropical planting often depends upon nearby plants that support and/or weave through it—creating an atmosphere or creating a backdrop. If it's just turf, the planting—though colorful—can look out of place.

Garden Beds

Seeing *Xanthosoma aurea* 'Lime Zinger' unfurling in a traditional garden bed changed my mind about tropical foliage, and I am thankful to the gardening friend who used a careful hand to showcase this outstanding plant among other temperate plants. It allowed me to observe the extraordinary shape, color, and vigor of the elephant ear, and in turn transfer that energy to the rest of the garden under a hot summer sun.

With the notable exception of tropically themed gardens, I have found that a careful, deliberate approach to using tropicals within garden beds is the most successful—particularly for beginners.

Within the existing framework of your temperate plants, assess your garden bed and ask yourself what you still need. Color? Height? Contrast? Dramatic accent? Do you wish to enhance or hide another feature, such as a wall, fence, or plant? The most successful design will have your visitors asking curious questions about individual, stunning plants. "Is it hardy? Is that really a banana? How do you overwinter it? Do the hummingbirds like it?"

Conversely, a sudden, solid wall of tropical foliage in a temperate garden feels unachievable, incongruous, and highly maintained—much like the massed Victorian tropical bedding plants of the late nineteenth century. Visitors may appreciate it, but nothing stands out, and the effect is often garish. I still see these displays particularly in public parks and remember the days when I didn't appreciate tropical plants—and why.

Instead, give visitors familiar touchpoints and stun them at the same time: *Hydrangea paniculata* 'Baby Lace' with a parrot heliconia (*Heliconia psittacorum*); *Canna* Tropicanna® emerging from the wispy, illuminated threads of *Miscanthus sinensis* 'Morning Light'; a majestic red Abyssinian banana standing sentry at a fork in the path, with a battalion of white, feathery cosmos at its knees.

Have fun mixing temperate and tropical plants together. And when the situation calls for more tropical than temperate, know a well-placed temperate perennial, shrub, or grass can often have a softening influence on the "shock and awe" effect of tropicals *en masse*.

By hiding the long, plain legs of *Hedychium coccineum* 'Tara,' temperate *Helenium* 'Moerheim Beauty' emphasizes and complements its exquisite orange heads in this expert combination at Great Dixter, Sussex, UK.

The Art of Pot Plunging

Many designers and experienced gardeners who use tropical plants in the landscape like to use the technique of plunging plastic pots into holes in the ground for the season.

Feeder roots will eventually grow through the drainage holes and out into soil depending on the size of the pot and the size of the plant, but plants will still need a little more attention from the hose.

There are many reasons why you may want to try this method in your own garden.

POT PLUNGING CAN WORK WELL FOR TEMPERATE GARDENERS AS A WAY TO:

- Protect tubers against hungry rodents.

- Create less root disturbance in the spring for tropicals started early under glass or in cold frames.

- Create a semi-permanent framework for designs you wish to repeat.

- Insulate pots from some water loss.

- Simplify fall chores for the gardener.

- Protect tubers, corms, and rhizomes from breakage.

- Create less root disturbance and leaf loss in the fall for greenhouse-wintered or garage-wintered plants kept in leaf.

This *Euphorbia milii* has been plunged in its pot for the season, making it easy to pull up and store in the autumn.

Three pots of *Sansevieria trifasciata* create contrast plunged into a bed of Japanese painted ferns (*Athyrium niponicum*) for the season.

Simply dig a hole the size of the pot, plunge the pot, and "plant it," backfilling the hole. If rodents are a problem, keep the lip of the pot proud of the hole by 2 inches (5 cm), which usually discourages them.

I have met designers who grow dahlias in simple 4-inch (10-cm) pots this way, and statement-makers that do not use any bromeliad under 3 gallons (11.4 L). This is the only way I grow my dahlias, for voles love them as much as I do.

For designs you love and plan to repeat, nesting a pot within a pot is a clever, easy idea, though plants aren't as insulated as they are against soil. Find a rigid nursery pot to act as a permanent placeholder and another pot that nestles within it for the plant itself. Dig a hole for the placeholder pot, keeping the lip of the pot flush with soil level, and plunge the other pot with plant inside it for the season.

At the end of the season, stand on the edges of the placeholder pot, so it doesn't shift, and lift up the inner pot, twisting it slightly as you lift to break any feeder roots.

CREATING PRIVACY

It's a very human desire to want to create spaces within our gardens that give us a sense of privacy and seclusion and keep the rest of the world at a distance when we need to.

By virtue of large foliage and fast growth patterns, tropical plants can help you achieve those spaces quickly, transforming a suburban patio into an intimate island getaway by mid-season.

Gardeners tend to think in terms of walls, fences, or tight hedges when considering options for privacy, but the truth is, we often only need a suggestion of height and mass to create a sense of enclosure. Two or three cleverly placed pots or a stand of *Canna* or banana in just the right place won't look like a barricade but can function as a visual barrier to prying eyes.

Here's where some of your containerized, larger-specimen Long-Term Commitments or High-Maintenance Partners can instantly help. (Remember to transition them slowly to higher light levels.) Palms, *Schefflera*, *Ficus*, *Monstera*, and *Dracaena* provide decorative privacy anchors that can be supplemented with other containers or garden shrubs to create a layered effect.

Large temperate grasses are particularly good partners in privacy, as they soften hard vertical lines while adding substantial presence to the overall effect. The wispy, rustling qualities of ornamental grasses also provide the sensual elements of movement and sound, which happily persist long after the season is over for their tropical companions.

Adding strung lights and a few lanterns capitalizes on the island feeling and allows you to see your guests. It also draws your view inward—away from neighborhood lights and distractions.

Assess where you need the most privacy—from a nosy neighbor on your right side . . . from an ugly view on your left. Sit in the chairs you will sit in and see how the view changes and possibly becomes more enclosed.

Then, set aside the idea of creating stiff, awkward boundaries with rigid lines of plants and think in terms of layering to create a relaxed boundary that feels more natural.

Purple hyacinth vine *(Lablab purpurea)* creates a simple, inexpensive, and beautiful border in a front garden. Given a taller fence to climb, this vigorous seed-reared Summer Romance will create almost instant privacy during the growing season.

Along with temperate shrubs, *Canna* and castor bean create a sense of privacy in this sunken patio from the subdivision homes that surround it. (Walser Garden, Brunswick, Maryland)

SUMMER STRUCTURE FOR YOUNG GARDENS

Just moved in? With fertile soil and adequate water, tropicals can give your new garden, patio, or deck almost instant gravitas, but the gardener must be careful not to completely rely on these temporary exotic bones—unless of course they are specifically creating an exotic garden.

There are many tropical plants that create structure, fast. *Canna*, bananas, *Colocasia*, castor bean, papaya, etc. . . . Use them to make your two-dimensional space a three-dimensional garden while your temperate plants are still small, making sure that you are not shading, or otherwise impeding, the growth of plants that will eventually make up the bones of your garden.

The wonderful thing about using tropicals this way is that they are temporary designs. As most gardeners learn over time, we rarely have the same plans (or plants!) for our garden after living with it for a few years.

You may find that the large stand of bananas in a corner is not as effective as a few dotted down a garden path, or that a small pond is overwhelmed by your collection of *Colocasia* cultivars and could really use a few water lilies instead.

Allow yourself to experiment, and don't be afraid to edit.

The area around this preformed pond in early summer betrays just how new it is.

Just five weeks later, carefully selected tropical plants both within and without have grown quickly and given the area a sense of permanence while slower-growing temperate plants begin to take hold.

Repetitive punches of contrasting color from the leaves of *Pennisetum* 'Black Stockings' break up a green tropical and temperate mix with refreshing contrast. (Chanticleer Garden, Wayne, Pennsylvania)

A TROPICALLY THEMED GARDEN

Some gardeners want to bring the island look back home in a big way—or just have an exotically themed garden in one part of a larger space. Though I don't choose to have a fully tropical garden, I am energized by these atmospheric spaces and enjoy visiting them tremendously.

If an exotically themed garden is what you've dreamed of, make it a little easier on yourself by researching what I call "Mocktrops"—plants that are hardy in your climate but look extremely tropical due to leaf size, flower, foliage contrast, etc. . . . Indeed, many of these plants may be exceptionally hardy tropicals, such as *Musa basjoo*. If you don't have much help in the garden, think about building 60 to 70 percent of the garden upon the backs of these plants and using your true tropicals as exciting, unusual accents to complete the picture.

Life happens, and sometimes you don't have the energy or time to deal with your tropical plants in the autumn. If they are Summer Romances, that's fine. If they make up 100 percent of your garden, you will have an expensive spring—or a breakdown.

Hardy Mocktrops can restore your vision, and your sanity.

As all bitter gardeners know, the term "hardy" usually reflects the climate of the gardener who's pronouncing judgment. That's why it's a great idea to get out and see gardens and gardeners in your area for Mocktrop ideas.

When visiting, note the plants that are creating a tropical atmosphere, and also take note of the site and exposure if they're growing vigorously. *Some Mocktrops may be invasive in your area*—it's why they're growing so well. Research carefully.

The author near a gigantic leaf of *Petasites japonicus* (butterbur) at her home in Virginia. Though highly tropical looking, this hardy Mocktrop can be invasive in some areas.

A collection of large-leafed Mocktrops and hardy tropicals, including *Rodgersia*, *Ligularia*, *Zingiber mioga*, and various ferns, creates a lush semi-tropical effect in the author's garden.

A Few Mocktrops to Interview*

Plant	Hardiness to
Acanthus mollis	-10°F (-23°C)
Albizia julibrissin	-10°F (-23°C)
Amorphophallus konjac	-10°F (-23°C)
Arisaema ringens	-20°F (-29°C)
Arundo donax 'Peppermint Stick'	-10°F (-23°C)
Begonia grandis	-10°F (-23°C)
Bergenia cordifolia	-40°F (-40°C)
Catalpa bignonoides 'Aurea'	-20° (29°C)
Clerodendron bungeii	0°F (-18°C)
Colocasia 'Pink China'	0°F (-18°C)
Crinum bulbispermum	-10°F (-23°C)
Darmera peltata	-20°F (-29°C)
Equisetum hyemale	-30°F (-34°C)
Eucomis comosa	-5°F (-21°C)
Farfugium japonicum var. *giganteum* 'Marco'	5°F (-15°C)
Fatsia japonica	0°F (-18°C)
Gunnera manicata	5°F (-15°C)
Hibiscus moscheutos	-20°F (-29°C)
Kalopanax septemlobus	-30°F (-34°C)
Ligularia dentata 'Othello'	-40°F (-40°C)
Manihot grahamii	5°F (-15°C)

Plant	Hardiness to
Matteuccia struthiopteris	-40°F (-40°C)
Metapanax delavayi	0°F (-18°C)
Musa basjoo	-15°F (-26°C)
Passiflora incarnata	0°F (-18°C)
Paulownia tomentosa	-20°F (-29°C)
Petasites japonicus	-20°F (-29°C)
Podophyllum pleianthum	-15°F (-26°C)
Rheum palmatum 'Atrosanguineum'	-10°F (-23°C)
Sabal minor 'McCurtain'	-5°F (-21°C)
Sauromatum venosum 'Indian Giant'	-10°F (-23°C)
Silphium terebinthinaceum	-40°F (-40°C)
Symplocarpus foetidus	-30°F (-34°C)
Syneilesis aconitifolia	-40°F (-40°C)
Tetrapanax papyrifer 'Steroidal Giant'	0°F (-18°C)
Tinantia pringlei	0°F (-18°C)
Trachycarpus fortunei	5°F (-15°C)
Zantedeschia aethiopica 'White Giant'	0°F (-18°C)
Zingiber mioga 'Dancing Crane'	-10°F (-23°C)

*Some Mocktrops may be invasive in your climate. Make sure you check a plant's status before using it.

In drier climates, containerizing tropicals makes sense, particularly bromeliads, which will hold a certain amount of water in their cup-like rosettes. Pictured: *Neoregelia kautskyi*. (Bullis Bromeliads, Princeton, Florida)

Navigating Rockier Relationships

While many temperate gardeners who suffer high heat and humidity levels in the summer will find that tropical plants are made for the needs of their punishing climates, gardeners in cooler or drier climates must work strategically to grow some of these plants well.

Aligning plant choices with your specific limitations is crucial, as is managing your expectations. For instance, gardeners with cooler summers may not be able to grow a 6-foot (1.8 m) *Colocasia*, but they'll be able to grow a 3-foot (1 m) *Colocasia*—and that's still a beautiful plant, especially when the humidity is so low that you can visit it in the middle of the day without passing out from heatstroke.

USE YOUR MICROCLIMATES AND MOCKTROPS IN COOLER CLIMATES

Understand the microclimates on your property and use them to your best advantage. Reflective walls, southern slopes, courtyard microclimates, large containers, and small bodies of water or paved surfaces can give your tropical plant an added boost of heat.

Use those Mocktrops to build a lush exotic feel, and get started as early as possible indoors with dormant rhizomes and corms.

Sauromatum venosum 'Indian Giant.' This exotic Mocktrop can tolerate temperatures of -10°F (-23°C), but looks like you must have overwintered it indoors. (Harper Garden, Seaford, Virginia)

CONTAIN YOUR TROPICALS IN DRY CLIMATES WITH POORER SOILS

Using tropicals as high-value container accents can solve regional problems. Soil and fertility can be customized, and containers can be strategically positioned to take advantage of existing drip systems so prevalent in dry climates.

Siting containers in shadier locations may help your plants to cope with humidity levels in the 10 to 25 percent range. Using *Canna* and *Colocasia* in containers as small water features can also provide a boost of humidity to other tropicals located close by.

KNOW WHERE YOUR WATER COMES FROM

If a beautiful range of mountains is your backdrop, the chances are high your water comes from snow melt. Ice cold water can set back or damage some tropical plants, such as *Caladium*. Set out watering cans overnight to avoid this hidden pitfall.

Other plants, such as *Cordyline*, can be badly affected by fluoridated water. If you're in a dry summer climate with little rainfall, that daily dose of the hose could be the reason you're experiencing leaf or growth difficulties.

GROW WHAT WORKS FOR YOUR SUMMER

Not everything will—even when other factors such as heat and humidity are in play.

For instance, hot, scorching winds can destroy the appearance of larger, leafy tropicals like *Colocasia* or *Alocasia*. Experiment with hardier tropical plants that can cope with challenging wind conditions, such as *Lantana*, *Verbena*, *Pentas*, and false vervain. You'll get a different tropical vibe with great flower color and save yourself a lot of tears.

Working with the species that work for your region takes experimentation and communication with great nurseries and plantspeople in your own area.

Some tropical flowers will give you constant color in the midst of extreme challenges—such as scorching winds. Pictured: *Pentas lanceolata* Graffiti® Bright Red. Photo credit: Steve Owens

RESEARCH YOUR FAVORITE PLANTS

Even if a tropical plant is hardy in your climate, it may not be able to reach its full potential within the parameters of that climate.

And the reasons why may be more nuanced than average annual rainfall, or average temperatures. Your nighttime temperatures can have a profound effect on the blooming and/or fruiting potential of your tropical plants, as can day length, and the amount of days above or below a certain temperature. If you're having issues, do more research into where, exactly, that plant comes from, and what it needs. You may be able to provide a work-around, or learn to enjoy it for what it does give you.

CAREFULLY OBSERVE TRUE MOISTURE NEEDS

If you live in a warm climate that can overwinter many subtropicals and hardier tropicals, congratulations! Your plants won't be forced to go through the trauma of digging, storage, and reestablishment. Established plants are stronger, more resilient plants. And this means their water needs are lessened.

While tropical plants will almost always require more water than their temperate cousins, it may be less than you think. Observe your plants carefully and you may be able to save water in an arid climate.

NEVER TAKE ANYTHING FOR GRANTED

If your last frost date is usually quite late, but increasingly unreliable, keep your eyes on your ten-day forecast and work toward containerizing some tropical displays and keeping them in cold frames or mini-hoop houses for full protection until the coast is truly clear. This will kick the heat up and provide instant impact when they're finally brought out later in the spring.

When winter doesn't want to end around here, I can increase the height on my straw bale cold frames with extra bales as plants grow, helping them (and me!) to weather an unpredictable season.

It's impossible to predict what spring has in store—as this photo taken on the first day of spring in the author's garden illustrates. Keep an eye on your ten-day forecast.

Relationship Fatigue

It's. So. Over.

Very few gardening books come with an exit strategy. This one does.

When you're growing something over many seasons that cannot survive in your climate without your intervention and care, it can become burdensome. That's why we must constantly re-examine our relationships with our tropical plants in terms of where we garden and our own life circumstances. This means:

- Our time

- Our energy

- Our budget

- Our life events

- Our climate and its resources

Life changes. And we need our plant choices to adapt.

Practically, it's something we should do on a consistent basis with our temperate gardens as well. Life changes, whether suddenly or gradually, and we need our gardens—and our plant choices—to adapt.

Though the relationship categories I have outlined in this book are fun, and definitely memorable (and I will no doubt take some ribbing for them in loftier plant circles), they serve another purpose. They allow us to confidently work with tropical plants on our own terms, knowing what they need, and what we can give.

We don't have to keep doing the same thing every year with the same plant. Editing and deleting not only refreshes our garden but also refreshes our spirit—giving us a needed break or providing an opportunity to work with new plants in new ways.

In temperate climates with winters below 0°F (-18°C), all of these tropical plants will need to be brought in for the winter. That's a lot of work year after year. (St. James Park, London, UK)

It's Not You. It's Me.

I find a great deal of joy in working with plants in all five of the relationship categories that we have discussed in this book. But over the years I have continually adjusted and readjusted what I'm willing to do, and plants have changed categories.

My skill level has also grown, so a plant that would have taken more of me ten years ago, takes very little of me now. It's a very cool thing to watch a High-Maintenance Partner turn into a Long-Term Commitment.

Along with an increased skill level comes an increased wisdom level (well, at least in some areas of my life). I know my limits where I once refused to see them—and got myself into unnecessarily stressful situations.

So, I definitely grow more Summer Romances these days, as I save much of my travel for the winter, when my temperate garden will let me get away and my Long-Term Commitments can handle a week or two without care. My Best Friends never know I left.

And whereas I might have dug every single rhizome of those sturdy Best Friends in autumn and faced a huge amount of repotting and relocation for plants in spring, I now ask myself before I dig, "How many do you really want?" and stop digging when I hit that number. I know myself well and know that if I dig them, I cannot let them perish in the spring for lack of a home.

Better to leave them outside in autumn and let Nature sort it out.

In contrast, this stunning combination in a garden that doesn't drop below 5°F (-15°C) in the winter may look very tropical but, in reality, cleverly relies on only one plant to migrate for the winter. Can you guess which one? (Mill Pond Garden, Lewes, Delaware)

Go big—or charm with just a flourish. You don't have to go "all in" to use tropical plants successfully in your temperate garden. (Garden of Barbara Katz, London Landscapes LLC)

Don't Get Carried Away

It's a good possibility that, once you work with tropical plants, and see what they can add to your garden and your home, you will overwhelm yourself within a few years. Passionate gardeners tend to jump into things with both feet—and these are seriously beautiful plants.

Fall and spring workloads aside, there can be a tipping point indoors where the plants we must walk around, reach over, take baths with, and occasionally find in our cornflakes can have a negative effect on our state of mind. It's important to figure out what that tipping point is for you—not what it might be for someone else.

Indoor plants beautify our lives and contribute to better mental and physical health. They make sense. *But if you're feeling overwhelmed* by a steadily growing collection, striking a balance between space and love/obsession is in order. It might be time to turn some of those Long-Term Commitments back into Summer Romances—or give them to an enthusiastic friend.

Be honest with yourself, with your space, and with your plants. Give them room to be their best and your indoor spaces will reflect that energy during some of the hardest months of the year.

Here are ten suggestions for moving slowly and keeping your garden, your home, and your workload balanced:

It doesn't cost much to sow a few tropical seedlings each year, but it can make a big impact on your garden without making a big impact on your life.

1. Aim to use tropical plants as *accents* in your temperate garden, not as the *framework* of your garden.

2. To create a tropically themed garden, use more Mocktrops—plants that give the same look but are fully hardy in your climate.

3. Give yourself a strict budget for a few exciting Summer Romances each spring. Stay within it.

4. While sowing your temperate vegetables and flowers, sow a few Summer Romances, such as castor bean or papaya, to fill space with tropical vigor at a tiny cost.

5. Use your container Summer Romances wisely, filling your pots with temperate annuals that accentuate the best of the tropical centerpiece.

6. Be completely honest about your indoor space restrictions. Don't crowd yourself.

7. Look for Long-Term Commitments that, first, will work well in your house; second, will work well on your patio.

8. Try out only one or two High-Maintenance Partners each autumn, so that you learn from the plant, but don't have so many to care for that you lose the point of the exercise.

9. Situate all of your tropical plants near an easy water source or in naturally moist areas of your garden. Having to water by hand gets old quickly. If you live in a dry climate, strategically use containers to get the most impact from the fewest plants.

10. Grow more Friends with Benefits than pure Summer Romances. Friends with Benefits not only are ornamental but also provide food value. That's a fun motivator during the growing season.

If you grow tired of your "tropical to-do list" every autumn, it's a good sign that things need to change and it's time to step back. It would be a shame to stop using tropical plants completely because you let your workload get out of control. Fine-tune it instead.

Here's to a Colorful and Adventurous Relationship!

Our gardens should enrich us—satisfying the artist, the cook, the creative, and the academic that lurks within all gardeners.

I, and many others, have delighted in using tropical plants to achieve this end, and I very much hope you will join us by dipping your brush into this incredible plant palette and using it to paint your garden with broad, beautiful strokes.

THE PLANTS
PREFACE

In these pages you will find profiles of tropical plants that I have found to be excellent choices for those getting started, those who have worked with tropical plants for a couple years, or those who love their houseplants and want to give them a new outdoor life.

These plants are listed by their genus (see page 34, Using Botanical Names), although in five cases (gingers, bananas, palms, elephant ears, and bromeliads), I have grouped them by their family name to make it as easy as possible for the reader to make connections between genera. An English respelling pronunciation is provided. Some lesser used but notable plants that deserve more text, but sadly cannot be spared any, are found at the end under "Don't Let Them Get Away" (page 194).

The plant icons, with which you have now become familiar, are added to each profile for easy reference, and represent my suggestions—*not my orders*—for growing and enjoying them. Never forget that you can enjoy *every single one* of these plants as a fabulous Summer Romance. Like all romances, some are more expensive than others.

Some genera have edible species. If so, the Friends with Benefits icon is also displayed, and the species and plant parts that are edible will be discussed. *Not all plants within a genus are edible.* Read carefully, and never try anything you are not 100 percent sure of.

This list is not comprehensive, but as it is not an encyclopedia—it cannot be. Therefore, I urge you to visit the Resources section (page 198) for more books on the subject and let the knowledge you have built here guide you in finding new and exciting love affairs that will fit your life and your limits.

If you see a plant you want to grow and cannot find it at your garden center, ask them to carry it. Tropical plants are gaining popularity rapidly, and it is very possible that they may order it for you. The modern gardener has been blessed by the incredible shopping tool that is the internet—use it.

Aglaonema

(ag-lay-oh-NEE-muh)

COMMON NAME: Chinese evergreen

LIGHT: Light shade to full shade

NATIVE TO: Southeast Asia

POTENTIAL PESTS/DISEASE: Thrips, mites; root and crown diseases if kept too wet

GREAT AS A: Long-Term Commitment

Aglaonema is easy to love long term. First, there's the large, variegated foliage. It's delicate but shiny; colorful in stem and leaf, but easily paired—creating a lush statement that works well outdoors in shade, or indoors in lower light conditions. *Aglaonema* are understory plants in their native subtropical habitat and benefit from rich, moist soils. They will burn quickly if exposed to direct sun. Leaves are usually ovate, deeply veined, and often speckled or marginated in contrasting colors of white, silver, pink, red, green, and orange.

Aglaonema Jazzed Gems™ 'Crosby's Christmas' gives you several colors to pull out when choosing complementary plants.

Red *Aglaonema* don't come much redder than cultivar 'SRA.'

Indoors, *Aglaonema* can handle slightly brighter light, but shouldn't be put next to a window, where temperature fluctuations can negatively affect them. They benefit from extra humidity, but overall are extremely tough. Nesting several contrasting plants together on a pebble tray is an attractive way of displaying and caring for them. Allow the soil to dry a little between waterings, but do not allow them to dry out completely—yellow leaves will result.

Indoors or out, most *Aglaonema* are slower growing and often have a full, shrubby appearance with multiple stems in the pot. Some species/cultivars can grow up to 48 inches (1.2 m) tall, but most grown indoors hover around 18 to 24 inches (45 to 61 cm)—perfect for a desk or table. Outdoors, use them where your sun-loving tropical foliage plants would reach and stretch.

For many years, the cultivar to grow was 'Silver Queen'—a fine plant with silver-gray leaves beautifully smudged with deep green veins and margins; now, red *Aglaonema* have taken over the market, with pink and red stems to match their fascinating, colorful leaves. Try 'Red Emerald' with deep red ribs to give you just a hint of color, or 'Crosby's Christmas' or 'Sparkling Sarah' for heightened reds. 'SRA' has recently excited growers as one of the reddest cultivars on the market. Fans of classic yellow/green or white/green variation are sure to love the lanceolate leaves of 'Cutlass' or the long, ovate leaves of 'Silver Bay' or 'White Calcite,' which give you variation without too much of a color commitment.

The deep black veining and unusual cupped appearance of *Colocasia* 'Coffee Cups' make them a gardener favorite. (Aldrich Garden, Alexandria, Virginia)

Elephant Ears (Araceae)

GENERA DISCUSSED: *Colocasia, Alocasia, Xanthosoma*

LIGHT: Part shade to sun

NATIVE TO: Tropical Asia, Australia, Tropical U.S., Central and South America

POTENTIAL PESTS/DISEASE: Aphids, Japanese beetles, mealy bug

GREAT AS A: Best Friend or High-Maintenance Partner

With fertile soil and adequate moisture, the leaves of *Xanthosoma aurea* 'Lime Zinger' can reach epic proportions.

Lush, vigorous elephant ears are a gardener's Best Friend in more ways than one. They not only provide striking, unusual foliage accents for containers, ponds, or beds, but after a winter in a dark frost-free space, come back better than ever. Each year I think I've seen them all, and then another hybrid hits the market and my collector's heart does a flip.

Not every genus in the Araceae family is an elephant ear, but they are all aroids—plants whose inflorescence consists of a spadix and spathe. Unless you grow your plants in ideal conditions, you may never see these hooded blooms—it took a monumental rainfall year to spot them in my garden.

No matter—elephant ears are all about the leaves. The common name refers to several genera (and hundreds of species and cultivars) that are characterized by large (up to 5 foot [1.5 m]) arrow or heart-shaped leaves, heavily veined, and held on the end of a long, sometimes colorful petiole that emerges from a large corm. Some are surprisingly hardy, such as *Colocasia esculenta* (5°F [-15°C]) and *Alocasia* 'Architexture,' which can survive many nights below freezing. But most are fairly tender, and require lifting.

Because there are some differences to growing (and storing) *Colocasia, Alocasia,* and *Xanthosoma*, it's good to know what you have; and because *really* knowing what you have involves a microscope and a knowledge of arum ovaries, we'll talk in generalities.

Colocasia 'Morning Dew' is richly patterned with dew-like splotches.

The petioles of some elephant ears are as remarkable as the leaves. Here, *Alocasia lutea*. (Pinkham Garden, Carrollton, Virginia)

In general, the leaves of *Colocasia* species point downward, the petiole is attached slightly in from the leaf notch, and the leaves are softer and often splotched or suffused with color. They tend to prefer sunnier and wetter environments and the round corms easily break dormancy in spring. Pink-petioled 'Pink China' also shows marked hardiness, though this may be due to its ability to produce numerous tiny cormels that beat the odds. Some of my favorite cultivars: 'Morning Dew,' 'Mojito,' 'Coffee Cups,' 'Fontenesii,' and 'Pharaoh's Mask.'

In general, *Alocasia* leaves tend to point upward (a notable exception is the fascinating *A. sanderiana*). The petiole is attached very near to the leaf notch, and the leaves are extremely sturdy, displaying pronounced veining. Partial to full shade conditions are appreciated and overwatering is discouraged. *Alocasia* is not thrilled about going into full dormancy, which is not a natural state, and takes some time to wake up. If you're going to keep a lit garage cool but not cold, or wish to battle aphids in your living room—this is one of the plants to do it for. *Alocasia* will ever-so-slowly diminish in size if not allowed to stay in leaf. My favorites: 'Tiny Dancers,' 'Sting Ray,' and the glorious, golden stemmed *A. lutea*.

In general, the arrow-shaped leaves of *Xanthosoma* point outward and downward. The large leaves also display a pronounced "collecting vein" that runs around the leaf margin—sometimes two (though a light vein is also present in *C. esculenta*). *Xanthosoma* break dormancy slower than *Colocasia* and faster than *Alocasia* and a dappled shade site is preferred. My journey to tropicals began with a cultivar of *X. aurea* 'Lime Zinger'—I hope to never be without it. *Xanthosoma atrovirens* 'Albomarginatum' is a fascinating white blotched variety with a curious tip "cup" and a taxonomic identity crisis. Search for *Xanthosoma* 'Albomarginatum' and you should be able to find it.

Colocasia esculenta (taro) is an edible staple in many countries—as is the lesser available *Xanthosoma sagittifolium*—but care must be taken in the preparation of both. Leaves contain high quantities of calcium oxalate crystals and must be boiled until tender before eating (about 45 minutes). Peeled corms can be thinly sliced into chips, but also must be cooked thoroughly before consuming. Use gloves when preparing!

Palms (Arecaceae)

GENERA DISCUSSED: *Howea, Rhapis, Chamaedorea, Butia, Trachycarpus, Sabal, Rhapidophyllum*

LIGHT: Part shade to sun

NATIVE TO: Subtropical and tropical regions worldwide

POTENTIAL PESTS/DISEASE: Spider mite, scale

GREAT AS A: High-Maintenance Partner

Trachycarpus fortunei is one of the hardiest palms, and with protection, can be grown where winter temperatures dip down to 5°F (-15°C). Photo credit: Kevin Prall

The palm family is vast and well beyond the scope of this book. However, the species that can tolerate a winter indoors is not. Therefore it is worth picking them out and providing a few tips for a better relationship—albeit a High-Maintenance one. Decide on the look you're going for—whether it's feathery leaves held upright, a classic "palm tree" appearance, or just a hint of Victorian parlor.

Palms form single trunks composed of old leaf bases, or they will be clumping—several stems to a pot. Most will be in a juvenile stage of growth when you buy them.

Most palms thrive in warm and moist conditions worldwide, with only a few genera adapting to desert conditions with the aid of deeper root systems and protective leaf cuticles. Brought indoors to dry, warm conditions, they will most likely struggle and be attacked by spider mites and scale once the honeymoon period of a couple months is over. Keeping them moist, giving them as much sunlight as possible, and regularly treating for pests should take you to the finish line. If you're not looking for that exoticism and neurosis over the winter, putting them into "stasis" in a cool, lit garage is perhaps a better idea, where the pressures of growing are lessened, as are pest populations.

Palms benefit more than most from a summer recuperation period. If you've got a dappled shade site, they will appreciate the extra water, sunlight, and humidity, and will respond by unfurling new leaves. Just one can instantly transform a patio, but be very careful to transition it slowly. Scalding the leaves will necessitate an even longer recuperation period.

A containerized group of *Howea forsteriana*, or the majesty palm—one of the most popular palms at garden centers. (Dutch Plant Farm, Frederick, Maryland)

Howea forsteriana (kentia or majesty palm) is possibly the largest and best known of the indoor palms. It has wide, pinnate leaves that stretch impressively from the slowly forming trunk. It is also slow growing, but tolerant of difficult situations as long as that summer vacation is on the schedule.

Chamaedorea elegans (parlor palm) has a slender trunk with upright, graceful, pinnate leaves that consequently don't take up too much lower-level real estate in the living room.

Phoenix roebelenii (dwarf date palm) is for those who want the classic look of a palm tree with a dense crown. It also has a slender trunk (sometimes sold with multiple trunks), but with feathery, pinnate leaves. Treat it right and you could have edible, if fibrous, fruit.

Rhapis (lady palm)—both *R. excelsa* and *R. humilis*, are extremely popular indoor palms, with palmate leaves on clustering stems that give a fuller effect. It is slow growing and variegated cultivars do exist.

Last of the (easier) indoor palms is *Butia capitata* (jelly palm), which has a thick trunk, gray-green recurving leaves like feathers, and the ability to weather 12°F (-11°C) if grown outside. It may also fruit.

If you wish to experiment with outdoor palms with or without protection, *Sabal minor* (palmetto palm) and mounding *Rhapidophyllum hystrix* (needle palm) are extremely hardy to 0°F (-18°C). For the classic palm look, *Trachycarpus fortunei* (windmill palm) is hardy to 10°F (-9°C) and will severely struggle down to 0°F (-18°C). Protect them against winter if you are pushing those parameters. A sheltered position is also important.

Placed against a bright pink wall, the recurved grayish leaves of *Butia capitata* become a sculptural element in an artist's garden. (Pinkham Garden, Carrollton, Virginia)

Majesty palm can act as a softening element for strong foliage colors.

147

Begonia

(beh-GO-née-uh)

COMMON NAME: Begonia

LIGHT: Shade/part shade/sun

NATIVE TO: Asia, Central and South America, Africa

POTENTIAL PESTS/DISEASE: Whitefly, spider mite; fungal disease and rot if kept saturated

GREAT AS A: High-Maintenance Partner or Best Friend

Lovely and definitely luxurious. *Begonia luxurians.*

The genus *Begonia* reminds me of that eclectic-but-fashionable friend who can't be pinned down to any one style. One day sporting sophisticated patterns, the next, daring dresses in outrageously hot colors—she always pulls off the look with a delightful asymmetry. *Begonia* has that elegance, that quirkiness, and that zest for life—it's a genus of mostly shade-loving species that can work as easily as Best Friends as they can your most challenging High-Maintenance Partner.

Rhizomatous species are characterized by thick, creeping stems that break the soil surface and sometimes display strongly patterned and/or colored leaves in varying shapes. The flowers, held in large graceful clusters, may also be impressive. Colorful rex begonias fall into this group, as does the large and lush 'Lotusland' and the fascinating, trunking *B. carolineifolia*. They prefer shady conditions with morning sun and cannot tolerate being saturated. Store rhizomes in their pots above freezing.

Tuberous species are sophisticated, floral, and feminine. They flower continuously with sumptuous, succulent blooms in almost every color and form, and instantly glam a container—particularly trailing cultivars such as *B. boliviensis* 'Bonfire.' The elegant I'Conia® series is one of my favorites. They too prefer shady conditions and a soil that is moist but not wet. Tubers can be lifted and stored in damp sawdust.

Fibrous-rooted *Begonia* without tubers or rhizomes are both down-to-earth and divas. Popular cultivars, such as Dragon Wing® *Begonia* or BIG® series, get on with it in the garden, providing large, waxy leaves in green or plum, ever-blooming flowers in pink, red, or white, and an ability to tolerate some measure of sunlight. 'Canary Wings' is a chartreuse cultivar with vermilion flowers for shade.

Others in this group, such as *B. luxurians*, do exquisite things in the summer if kept happy with humidity, moisture, and shade, but will rapidly expire indoors if you are not doting. Angel wing *Begonia* hybrids with their patterned seraphic leaves are much easier and the relationship less likely to end in tears.

Begonia grandis is hardy to -10°F (-23°C)—an excellent Mocktrop.

above Fabulous, colorful foliage is the hallmark of rex begonias. Here, 'Dibs Cherry Mint.'

left A popular container begonia, Dragon Wing® with Proven Accents® 'Variegata' vinca.

For gardeners with winters above -10°F (-23°C), *B. grandis* adds Mocktrop exotica to the garden with blood-red undersides to green leaves and either white or pink flowering bracts.

Bromeliads (Bromeliaceae)

GENERA DISCUSSED: *Neoregelia, Alcantarea, Aechmea, Vriesea, Guzmania, Ananas, Tillandsia*

LIGHT: Part shade to sun

NATIVE TO: Tropical Americas

POTENTIAL PESTS/DISEASE: Remarkably resilient to pests

GREAT AS A: High-Maintenance Partner or Long-Term Commitment

The remarkable family that is Bromeliaceae comprises some of the most exciting and unusual tropical plants you can grow. They come in many sizes and make a spectacular foliage and floral impact in the garden and in the home. You can dabble by watching a pineapple (*Ananas*) develop as a fun Summer Romance; or by bringing a small, plastic-like *Guzmania* in the house; or by hanging an air plant (*Tillandsia*) from your bathroom mirror. But once you recognize how much they can add to the garden, you may find yourself making considerable winter living space available for a majestic *Alcantarea imperialis*. This is an addictive family, and when you find a nursery that specializes, it's like finding a candy store.

Bromeliads are plants that consist of leathery, sometimes spiny, often colorful leaves growing in a rosette pattern around a central core. There are both epiphytic and terrestrial species. Epiphytic species, with the exception of most *Tillandsia*, can be planted in a porous soil. Fertilize rarely—perhaps once a month during the growing season. Fish emulsion is my food of choice.

Bromeliads conveniently provide their own cups to catch a drink, and filling the cup is the easiest way of making sure they are getting the correct amount of water. Indoors you may do similarly, though if temperatures are cold (below 60°F [16°C]) this can cause rot. *Tillandsia* species should be dunked once a week until fully saturated and allowed to drain. Up the humidity levels where you can for all your indoor specimens.

All bromeliads flower once in their lifetime from the center of the plant, whether flamboyantly on tall stems, or quietly and delicately within the inner cup. The flower is usually very long lasting. Once a bromeliad has flowered, pups (or kikis) emerge from the base and the parent plant slowly

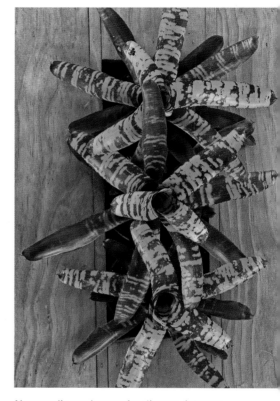

Neoregelia are known for diverse, intense coloring. Here, three 'Guacamole' form the sunken centerpiece in a creative coffee table. (Bullis Bromeliads, Princeton, Florida)

Another perfectly named cultivar—*Vriesea ospinae* var. *gruberi* 'Batik'

dies. Separate them carefully with a sharp knife and pot up when they have developed at least five leaves.

Many species cope well with full sun, though if you live in a warm climate, it is wise to give them some shelter from afternoon sun and to avoid reflective surfaces.

Species that enjoy partial shade or shade conditions are the compact and intensely colored *Neoregelia* ('Guacamole' is a favorite, as is 'Rubrovittata Fuego') and *Vriesea* (Try *V. ospinae* var. *gruberi* and *V. hieroglyphica*). Color in *Neoregelia* can be intensified in both part-shade and slightly sunnier positions, depending on cultivar, so experiment. You'll find that indoors, foliage colors may fade, only to reappear when the plant goes outside in spring.

The stunning inflorescences of sun-loving *Aechmea* are otherworldly, and beginners will adore the long-lasting violet iridescence of the popular cultivar 'Blue Tango' as well as the pink and blue inflorescence on the silver-foliaged *A. fasciata*. *Vriesea* also throw stunning, flattened flowers in a rainbow of colors.

A word on edible pineapples (*Ananas comosus*). Grown from pineapple tops, they may take up to two years to fruit on a spiny plant that can top out at 4 to 5 feet (1.2 to 1.5 m). That's High-Maintenance. Try a slightly smaller species such as the red pineapple (*A. bracteatus*), or its hybrids. Or start with pups or more mature plants that are ready to flower.

Bright and beautiful *Brugmansia insignis* 'Insignis Pink'

Brugmansia

(broog-MAN-see-uh)

COMMON NAME: Angel's trumpets

LIGHT: Full sun to partial sun

NATIVE TO: Tropical Andes regions of South America, often at high altitude

POTENTIAL PESTS/DISEASE: Spider mite, aphids, cabbage worm

GREAT AS A: Best Friend

Brought in every year, some *Brugmansia* can gain tree-like height and girth, creating strong anchors in the garden. (Garden of Kellie O'Brien, Chicago, Illinois)

Delicate but deadly, *Brugmansia* species are flowering, fragrant divas in the summer garden if their heavy feeding and drinking requirements are met. They also tolerate light frost and can be hardy to temperatures as low as 20° to 25°F (-6° to -4°C). Their strong perfume is most noticeable as the sun sets and the air grows heavy each evening.

Angel's trumpets is an excellent common name for a plant that is covered from mid-summer to fall with silken, funnel-like blossoms. The tips of the fused petals appear to be pulled up by invisible threads, and flowers open in variations of white, orange, yellow, and deep pink. Foliage is large, lightish-green, and somewhat coarse. Cultivars such as 'Maya' (aka 'Sunset'), 'Snowbank,' and 'Apricot Queen' display strong variegation.

Brugmansia is most commonly found in single forms (often as culti-vars of *B. versicolor)*, though double-flowered hybrids and cultivars of *B. x candida* are becoming more popular. 'Double White' and 'Double Apricot' are two imaginatively named cultivars. One of my favorite *B. versicolor* hybrids is 'Supernova White'—a single with pendulous, vertical blooms that rocks my fall garden with very little work on my part. Another favor-ite—*B. insignis* 'Insignis Pink' (syn. 'Frosty Pink')—leans deeply toward the rose end of the spectrum rather than the salmon.

Growth is that of a shrubby small tree—growing up to 30 feet (9 m) tall where it is hardy. In smaller specimens it will appear almost vase shaped, and therefore makes an excellent candidate for containers. *Brugmansia* has distinct vegetative and flowering stages, and generally will not start setting flower buds until it has reached a height of at least 3 to 5 feet (1 to 1.5 m), so be patient and keep feeding.

In the busy fall, *Brugmansia* makes a fabulous Best Friend. The plant can be dug, cut back to a strong framework, potted in fresh, moist potting soil, and stored in a dark, cool basement or garage. Cutting back too drastically can affect how long the plant will take to get out of the vegetative stage in the spring, but dieback might take that decision out of your hands.

All parts of *Brugmansia* and its cousin *Datura* (thorn apple) are extremely toxic and can be fatal.

Caladium

(ka-LAY-dee-um)

COMMON NAMES: Angel wings, elephant ear

LIGHT: Full shade to full sun

NATIVE TO: South America

POTENTIAL PESTS/DISEASE: Bulb rot, Southern blight, aphids

GREAT AS A: Summer Romance

Caladium are sold both as dormant bulbs (tubers) and as fully finished pots of heart- or arrow-shaped leaves supported by delicate stems. Though there are seven species within the genus *Caladium*, most of the cultivars available to home gardeners are bred from *C. bicolor*. Leaves come in every conceivable pattern in colors of white, green, red, and pink, and are generally split into two groups—fancy leaf (very shade tolerant) and strap leaf (very sun tolerant). Although I enjoy the charms of most cultivars, I especially value the white cultivars such as 'Allure,' 'Snow Drift,' and 'Moonlight' for the energizing effect they have on my shady patio and front step. 'Peppermint' is an artistic masterpiece.

Most gardeners underestimate this plant's need for *heat*. Early planted bulbs can rot waiting for soil to significantly warm. Understanding this is the key to understanding *Caladium*, and perhaps even taking this Summer Romance to the next level.

Avoid late-winter impulse buys of cardboard pictures stapled to bags of dry sawdust. Instead, buy #1 or larger bulbs from a reputable online supplier. In optimum conditions, with soil temperatures reliably at 65° to 70°F (18° to 21°C), those bulbs will become gorgeous plants in 10 to 12 weeks. Using containers with bottom heat makes this process faster. Good-quality potting mix or light garden soil and a sprinkle of slow-release fertilizer should provide all the nutrients your *Caladium* need for the season. If you're trying to bulk them up for next year, fertilize more heavily.

Buy full-grown plants when night temperatures are reliably warm and do not plant into still-cold soil. Water should be at room temperature.

One way to differentiate a sun-loving strap leaf from a shade-loving fancy leaf is to observe where the petiole (stem) hits the leaf. If it's in the center, it's most probably a fancy leaf. If it hits at the notch of the leaf, it's probably a strap leaf cultivar.

Storage of *Caladium* bulbs can be tricky, and is the reason I usually treat these striking plants as Summer Romances. Unlike *Canna* or *Colocasia*, they need storage temperatures of 60° to 65°F (16° to 18°C). If you've got an unused bedroom that stays very cool, experiment with some bulbs in a drawer!

Caladium are an excellent choice for window boxes in a dappled shade position.

Proven Winners® sun tolerant Heart to Heart™ *Caladium*.

Caladium 'Peppermint' and 'Summer Breeze' pair perfectly with *Peperomia obtusifolia* 'Variegata.'

The stately, blushed leaves of *C. musaefolia* in mid-summer. (Chanticleer Garden, Wayne, Pennsylvania)

Canna

(KA-nuh)

COMMON NAMES: Canna lily, Indian shot plant

LIGHT: Sun, partial shade

NATIVE TO: Southern Asia, Subtropical North and South America

POTENTIAL PESTS/DISEASE: Slugs and snails, spider mite, canna leaf roller, Japanese beetles, viral infections

GREAT AS A: Best Friend

Lemon & Gin™ Cabana Canna™® backed by the variegated leaves of Tropicanna® Gold.

Canna species epitomize the Best Friend relationship. The shallowly rooted rhizomes are easily dug and stored in cold zones, they grow quickly, and the highly variable plants offer the most versatility in the summer garden—growing in both sun and partial shade, in average soils and moist ones . . . or even submerged in water features. They are heavy feeders and benefit from rich soils and a sprinkling of slow-release fertilizer when potting up in early spring.

Canna are used as vertical accents in containers and beds—and can provide effective screening with large, ovate leaves that clasp the rigid stems, culminating in a flower spike of up to eight blossoms—though it is more often the foliage rather than the flower that draws you in. Flower spikes are easily deadheaded, and while the stem and leaves will remain, that shoot will not regrow or branch. New stems must come from below.

Viral disease is very common in vegetatively propagated canna (as opposed to seed-reared). Torn, ruffled, or streaked leaves are symptoms. It is best to dig and destroy affected plants to prevent spread.

Generally, the named cultivars easily available to home gardeners are lumped together under the species *C.* x *generalis*, and known simply by their cultivar name. 'Bengal Tiger' (syn. 'Pretoria'), 'Red Stripe,' 'Cleopatra,' 'Cosmopolitan,' 'Australia,' and 'Tropicanna®' are some of my favorites. But other species are worth seeking out, such as *C. musaefolia*—a stately 7-to-10-footer (2–3 m) with a pinkish cast to its stems, ribs, and banana-like leaves; or the blue-green leaves and apricot blooms of *C. glauca* 'Panache'—bred from the original species of aquatic *Canna*.

In containers, it is vital you match the height of your *Canna* to the rest of your arrangement—and avoid the proportion pitfall of many a container gardener. For small containers, choose one of the many dwarf cultivars (2 to 3 feet [60 to 90 cm]), such as 'Lemon & Gin™,' 'Flirtini®,' 'Aloha,' or one from the newish Cannova® series.

Canna indica (syn. *C. edulis*) is an edible canna species with large rhizomes grown as a starch crop in South America for millennia.

Codiaeum

(koh-die-EE-um)

COMMON NAME: Croton

LIGHT: Full sun to part shade

NATIVE TO: Moluku Islands of Eastern Indonesia

POTENTIAL PESTS/DISEASE: Spider mite, scale, anthracnose if overwatered

GREAT AS A: Summer Romance

'Dreadlocks' croton lives up to its name. (Vizcaya Museum and Gardens, Miami, Florida)

Over the last few years, growers have been introducing this high-contrast, high-impact foliage plant to temperate gardeners primarily as an autumn accent plant in preplanted containers. Color-wise, it makes sense. The yellows, oranges, and reds that suffuse the tough, leathery leaves are perfect on a New England porch in early September. That is, until the temperature drops a few weeks later. Crotons are quite sensitive to frost and will quickly drop leaves.

Why not get more out of your investment, buying them in the late spring, and treating them as exciting Summer Romances for containers, beds, patios, and decks? There's so much to explore. Croton leaves can be ovate, long and slender, thin and reedy, twisted, pendulous, and even oak-shaped.

Crotons are often planted in full sun, but those saturated colors are shown to their best advantage in a site with some shelter from afternoon rays. They make fantastic container plants, and if used as an anchor in a pot, can be transitioned with new autumn companions until the temperatures become too cold. Water regularly, but in a pot with excellent drainage.

Crotons are relatively slow growing, so if you've found a cultivar you love at a size you can handle, consider bringing them indoors as a High-Maintenance Partner. They'll need a higher level of indoor light, and soil that does not get too dry. Increased humidity is also appreciated. You will find that color fades in leaves with lower light levels.

Many hybrids sport color differences in juvenile and mature foliage, and are hybrids bred from *Codiaeum variegatum*. There is much to explore. 'Petra' is the can't-go-wrong classic, but once you've seen the twisted, elongated leaves of 'Mammy' or the long, flat shoestring leaves of 'Zanzibar,' you may no longer settle for common. 'Zanzibar' also works well in hanging baskets, as does 'Dreadlocks' (perfectly named). If you're looking for yellow/green hybrids, try 'Gold Star,' or 'Sunny Star'—the latter holds its yellow-green leaves in three-dimensional bunches. The unusual warm and cool variegation of both 'Yellow Iceton' and 'Red Iceton' will create a pretty spectacular container.

There are hardly any rules when it comes to crotons. Here, brilliant colors decorate the cultivar 'Oakleaf.'

Cordyline

(kor-dill-LIE-nee)

COMMON NAMES: Cabbage tree, ti plant

LIGHT: Full sun to partial shade

NATIVE TO: Southeast Asia, Australia

POTENTIAL PESTS/DISEASE: Spider mite, stem rot and various leaf spots, Southern blight; susceptible to fluoridated water

GREAT AS A: Summer Romance or High-Maintenance Partner

Cordyline fruticosa 'Harlequin' gives the clever container gardener a lot of colors to work with.

Garden centers and landscapers have overused rusty-red cultivars of *Cordyline australis* as the ubiquitous "thriller" plant for container designs for so many years that gardeners can be excused for not realizing that this is a genus made up of *truly* thrilling plants, many of which belong to the wider-leafed species *C. fruticosa* (syn. *C. terminalis*). *Cordyline* bring color, structure, and vigor to sunny or shady containers, beds, and borders with leaves 12 to 20 inches (30 to 51 cm) long; and can be dug and potted for a cool, light basement in winter, or tended with an eye to spider mite indoors. *Cordyline* are drought sensitive and very frost tender.

Though there are over twenty-five accepted species of *Cordyline*, exploring *C. fruticosa* cultivars is one of the best ways to fall in love with this dramatic, architectural plant, as their many colors can be expertly paired to bring out accents in containers, or bring a bright spark to an otherwise glum corner.

Cordyline adapt very well to sunny places, but they are most happy in a partially sunny site. It is vitally important that plants purchased in an indoor setting are gradually re-introduced to higher light levels outdoors.

You are most likely to find *Cordyline* as a single upright stem in a pot. If you're lucky, the pot will have two or three rooted stems, making a fuller plant, though you can prune low and stimulate the stem to throw new stems during the growing season. Festival™ is an exciting new series that grows multiple stems from the base when the crown is buried 1 to 2

Cordyline fruticosa 'Xerox' is a very popular cultivar whose psychedelic shades of pink will stand out in any landscape.

An old favorite, *Cordyline australis* adds a spiky accent to a collection of *Canna*. (Aldrich Garden, Alexandria, Virginia)

inches (2.5 to 5 cm) into the soil—giving the plant the look of *Pennisetum* or *Phormium*.

Vigorous growth and the eventual fading of lower leaves make pruning an inevitable choice. It is tough to cut a colorful, anchoring stem back to stimulate new growth, but when done carefully, it will create a better-looking plant. If you have several stems, stagger your cuts so new growth is not congested and looks natural. Tip cuttings can be rooted in water.

For fantastic kaleidoscope color, try *C. fruticosa* 'Harlequin' or the white-green-red mix of 'Kiwi.' Red lovers will appreciate 'Hot Pepper' and the much-planted Florida-faves 'Red Sister' and 'Xerox.'

Or just be traditional, and experiment with a *C. australis* in the middle of your petunias.

Fragrant shoots of lemongrass are prepared in the kitchen.

Cymbopogon

(sim-bow-PO-gon)

COMMON NAME: Lemongrass

LIGHT: Full sun

NATIVE TO: Subtropical and Tropical Africa and Asia

POTENTIAL PESTS/DISEASE: Spider mite, mealy bug, leaf rust

GREAT AS A: Best Friend

I consider ornamental grasses critical in bringing movement and sound into a garden (not to mention structure and wildlife habitat). Tropical lemongrass offers gardeners yet another gift: flavor. The crisp, lemony fragrance of lemongrass is familiar to fans of Southeast Asian food; and growing it fresh means you can up your game in the kitchen while enjoying its substantial, cooling presence in the garden. If you have a long season, you may have flowering panicles in the fall.

There are more than 100 species of *Cymbopogon*. The genus is grown extensively throughout the tropical and subtropical world for its powerful essential oil, which may be used for medicinal purposes and cosmetic fragrances—and the well-known insect repellent: citronella, distilled from the leaves of *C. nardus*.

The species most commonly used for Thai and Vietnamese cooking is *C. citratus*, whose rough blue-green leaves emerge from white stems at the base of the plant that eventually grow quite fat and separate. It is those bulbous, flavor-packed sections that are most often used for flavoring dishes. *C. flexuosus*, grown for essential oil, may also be used for cooking, but is not preferred.

One of the other benefits to *Cymbopogon* is in its ability to cope with poor soils in the garden, though it will not tolerate overly dry conditions for too long. As it is a fibrous-rooted plant that holds the soil well and grows quickly, it is often good to plunge a pot (of desirable size) in the ground for easy removal in the fall *before the frost*, where it can go in a dark garage or basement, trimmed and dormant, with the rest of your Best Friends. Do not allow it to go bone dry during the winter months or it will perish.

Lemongrass oil is used by beekeepers to bait swarm traps in mid-spring. It is extremely effective at getting scout bees to explore the trap and possibly move the colony in.

As the weather cools, lemongrass takes on rich purple tones.

Cyperus

(SIE-pur-us)

COMMON NAMES: Papyrus, umbrella palm, bullrush

LIGHT: Full sun

NATIVE TO: Madagascar

POTENTIAL PESTS/DISEASE: Spider mite

GREAT AS A: High-Maintenance Partner

The feathery heads of *C. papyrus* add a unique and exotic texture to the garden

If you're going to come under the spell of an exotic plant while browsing the sunny aisles of your garden center, papyrus in one of its many forms is a likely charmer. The strong green stems topped with tufts of wild hair are at once unusual and yet reminiscent of childhood adventure stories in ancient lands. New cultivar names play up this theme, and you may find one in your cart before you even realize what you've done.

The incredibly tall stalks (up to 13 feet [4 m]) and fine threads of *Cyperus papyrus* can be found under the species name, or under patented cultivars 'King Tut' (up to 72 inches [1.8 m]) or 'Prince Tut' (up to 30 inches [76 cm]).

If you're looking for smaller cultivars, be aware that you'll also end up with a slightly different appearance. 'Baby Tut' (up to 24 inches [61 cm]) is a *C. alternifolius* (syn. *C. involucratus*) dwarf cultivar whose bladed umbrella heads reflect the difference in species. *C. haspan* 'Cleopatra' is an 18 inches (46 cm) tall papyrus with heads shaped like stars, often used in container arrangements. For plant collectors, *C. albostriatus* 'Variegatus' is harder to find but just as easy to grow. At 24 inches (61 cm) tall, it wows with white accents.

Papyrus is primarily an aquatic plant that enjoys higher humidity but, given moisture-retentive soils and an attentive gardener, can tolerate garden beds. Consider using the larger species/cultivars as stand-alone statements in large, drainless tubs or terracotta pots lined with plastic inserts that can be easily filled with soil and water.

If you pamper a member of this royal family over the winter, be aware that cats eat it like Pringles® and a neglected plant will perish quickly. Plunge your prince or princess in a drain-free pot and keep it *wet and warm* over the winter near the sunniest window you have. Keep a sharp eye out for spider mite, which thrives in dry home conditions.

The common weeds nutsedge and nutgrass are actually *Cyperus* species. Look carefully when you're pulling and you'll see the family resemblance!

C. alternifolius with *Muehlenbeckia axillaris*
(Chanticleer Garden, Wayne, Pennsylvania)

Dahlia 'Tabasco'—sumptuous and sexy

Dahlia

(DAL-ya)

COMMON NAME: Dahlia

LIGHT: Full sun

NATIVE TO: Central America

POTENTIAL PESTS/DISEASE: Deer, voles, aphids

GREAT AS A: Best Friend

Dahlia 'Mystic Illusion' with *Xanthosoma aurea* 'Lime Zinger,' *Ensete ventricosum* 'Maurelii,' and *Miscanthus sinensis* 'Morning Light'

Dahlia meet the late-summer garden with color and intensity, and that's why I love them—particularly the cultivars that do so in hot, shameless shades of vermilion and tangerine. Nearing the end of the seasonal party, *Dahlia* pour another drink and settle in—asking a sunny position, adequate moisture, and a regular deadheading from the grateful gardener.

Though *Dahlia* do not have the drought tolerance of late-summer *Zinnia*, they can boast of finer, pinnate foliage as well as a vast diversity of bloom size and color. They are tuberous-rooted perennials that function beautifully as Best Friends, stored with just a hint of moisture in sawdust or soil.

I grow mine in gallon pots plunged deep in well-drained soil with the lip sitting proud to discourage hungry voles. After a killing frost I pull the pots and give the tubers the sawdust treatment, checking on them now and again to make sure the tubers are not shriveling.

In early spring, tuber clumps can be divided, but the divisions will not sprout if they do not have "eyes"—which usually form a collar around the stem section. You may not spot them readily—even the experts have trouble sometimes. Plant with the eyes upright and no more than 2 inches (5 cm) below the soil line. Cuttings may also be taken of a few new sprouts—but don't be greedy. Wait for sprouting to begin before watering and fertilizing.

In the garden, *Dahlia* can grow up to 5 feet (1.5 m) tall, and may require staking if wind is an issue. A dose of potassium nitrate when stems are budding can create a stronger framework, as can removing two pairs of leaves when you deadhead.

Frankly, volumes could be written, and have been. I will admit my bias toward single cultivars, which have a happy flamboyance about them that I find appealing—particularly the Mystic® and Happy Single® series with plum foliage.

The species *D. imperialis* is worth growing as an impressive foliage shrub that can give you 8 feet (2.4 m) of impact in a season, though you may be racing against your frost clock for blooms. Explore and experiment, and find yourself smitten.

167

Dracaena

(druh-SEE-nuh)

COMMON NAMES: Cornstalk plant, dragon tree

LIGHT: Shade to partial shade to sun

NATIVE TO: Tropical Africa, Madagascar, South America

POTENTIAL PESTS/DISEASE: Mealy bug, scale, stem rot, Southern blight

GREAT AS A: Long-Term Commitment

A vertical plant for living rooms, accenting a container, or plunging in the garden, *Dracaena* species add strong architectural accents with wide or thin strappy, lanceolate leaves, attractive trunks, and a spiky, shiny appearance. If pruned correctly, they can also form shrubby, multi-stemmed plants that will create strong foliage contrast in the garden. There are many variegated cultivars in shades of cream, yellow, white, and chartreuse—some with red margination.

Sun tolerance varies by species. Forest-dwelling wider-leaved species such as *D. fragrans* prefer lower light levels, while open scrub species like *D. marginata* are children of the sun. Both are remarkably drought-tolerant though *D. fragrans* prefers more moisture. All species respond equally well—if a little slowly—to a cut-back of gangly or awkward stems, but care must be taken to prune in a staggered height pattern to ensure a more pleasing re-flush.

D. marginata is perhaps the best known of the genus. Thin, supple, shiny green leaves have strong red margins and enjoy full sun; be sure to transition them slowly. 'Tricolor' has cream centers with wide red margins that verge on pink. They can get rangy—don't be fearful with the pruners.

For wide, softer leaves, and a tolerance for neglect, *D. fragrans* (syn. *D. deremensis*) favors mid- to low-light situations and eventually makes a large floor or patio specimen. It can be sensitive to very high temperatures but can flower fragrantly in ideal circumstances. 'Rikki' and 'Warneckii' are two of the best-known variegated cultivars; 'Lemon Lime' and 'Limelight' are even brighter. 'Harvest Moon' is an exciting new acid-green cultivar with thin deep green striations near the margins and a dramatic overall width.

The shorter, reflexed leaves of *D. reflexa* species are often variegated and lend themselves to creative pruning to create a fuller, shrubbier plant. Both 'Song of Jamaica' and 'Song of India' are two extremely attractive cultivars, with green-on-green and green-on-white variegation, respectively.

For the truly committed, *D. arborea* offers a stately appearance with a thick trunk and very wide, long leaves—low to mid-light preferred.

D. fragrans tops a colorful arrangement of *Neoregelia* and *Anthurium*.

D. fragrans 'Harvest Moon' will certainly show up in the garden by moonlight.

Epipremnum aureum 'Pearls and Jade' (lower left) and *Scindapsus pictus* (lower right) combine with *Dieffenbachia* and *Aglaonema* in a well-balanced container for a shady site.

Epipremnum

(eh-pe-PREM-noom)

COMMON NAMES: Pothos, devil's ivy

LIGHT: Shade, part shade

NATIVE TO: Southeast Asia

POTENTIAL PESTS/DISEASE: Very resilient to pests. Can suffer from a build-up of fertilizer salts in soil.

GREAT AS A: Long-Term Commitment

There is perhaps no easier Long-Term Commitment than *Epipremnum*. This one shares a pot with a *Sansevieria*.

When we crossed the country many years ago to settle in the mid-Atlantic, a small pot of pothos (*Epipremnum aureum*) sat at my feet—a parting gift from my mother. I still have that plant, which has sired countless others for both indoor and outdoor use over the years. Next to *Philodendron*, it is one of the most recognizable plants in the indoor jungle, with heart-shaped, golden-splotched leaves in many patterns and vigorous, vining stems that trail or climb. It's easy. It's durable. And all those prunings you keep taking can go outside to create a seasonal groundcover or attractive climbing plant—or simply fill more pots for friends and family.

One of the handiest things about *Epipremnum* generally is its ability to root both in water and at the leaf nodes in soil, which allows the gardener with a sense of timing to do major prunings just after the last frost, when lengths of stem can be laid on moist, shady soil, and lightly covered just to hold them down. With heat, the cuttings will root and spread, creating a tropical texture that is as cheap as it is attractive. Other cuttings can be used to make trailing accents for shady containers. In frost-free climates where it is hardy, it can become an invasive nuisance, which probably accounts for its other common name—devil's ivy.

There are distinct juvenile and mature stages to *Epipremnum*, which are characterized by leaf shape and size. Most garden center offerings are sold in a juvenile stage. *E. aureum*, the most popular species, has many excellent cultivars. 'Pearls and Jade' and 'Silver Queen' are two of my favorites, as I love cooler tones in mixed containers. Larger-leafed *E. pinnatum* develops fenestrations (windows) in its leaves in mature plants, and 'Variegata' is a new up and comer. 'Cebu Blue' has a longer, slender leaf in lovely shades of gray-blue.

Of a separate genus entirely, *Scindapsus pictus* is often called pothos in garden centers and the differences are small. 'Trebi' is a gorgeous cultivar that I include here just to be rebellious.

Epipremnum aureum can create a seasonal groundcover for a shady space.

Ficus

(FIE-cuss)

COMMON NAMES: Fig, fiddleleaf fig, rubber plant

LIGHT: Part shade to full sun

NATIVE TO: Southwest Asia, Mediterranean

POTENTIAL PESTS/DISEASE: Scale, spider mite

GREAT AS A: Long-Term Commitment

Ficus tikoua, a vigorous, highly attractive groundcover

Figs possess a strength and confidence that translates as well outdoors as it does inside. There are more than 800 species to the genus *Ficus*—a diverse group of occasionally hardy, sun-loving plants and trees. Eat the fruits, relish the structure, revel in the low upkeep.

With strong, leathery leaves and tolerance for indoor light levels, the fiddleleaf fig (*Ficus lyrata*) has recently knocked the more delicate weeping fig (*F. benjamina*) out of its decades-long dominance of interior design. Weeping figs notoriously lose their thin leaves in low-light or stressful conditions indoors (as does the new star, *F. triangularis* 'Variegata'). With all, stay consistent in your care and allow soil to dry out between waterings, regularly turning the plant to keep the shape strong.

F. elastica, the rubber plant, can also tolerate average light conditions, and its large, almost artificially glossy leaves will take on a deeper essence in lower light—though it might grow spindly. Prune occasionally to keep it tight, and wear gloves. All *Ficus* ooze milky sap that can be irritating to skin.

F. benghalensis 'Audrey' has ovate green leaves smaller than *F. elastica*, and a more open habit. 'Bengal Sun' is a chartreuse cultivar worth searching for, but as elusive as the Loch Ness Monster—I am thankful to a connected friend for a gifted plant. *All of the above must be slowly transitioned to outdoor conditions.*

Once outside, figs prefer well-drained soils and a sunny to partially sunny location. Humidity and moisture will encourage a growth spurt—too much wet will drown them.

Ficus lyrata growing happily under a Florida sun. They'll be transitioned to lower light levels for retail, but must be *slowly* transitioned back when placing outdoors.

A happy and healthy *Ficus elastica* on a shady porch in mid-summer

Climbing and creeping species add much to the temperate garden. *F. tikoua* needs at least 5°F (-15°C) over the winter, so I grow this large-leafed creeper as a Summer Romance. It grows exponentially and does something magical to a rocky outcrop. Ditto *F. pumila*—its curiously flattened leaves can cover a wall in seconds flat.

Of the edible species (*F. carica*)—'Brunswick', 'Brown Turkey', and 'Chicago Hardy' are the hardiest (at least -5°F [-21°C]). If they are root hardy for you (a south-facing wall is helpful), you may be able to pick plump, heavenly geodes before the first frost. In a cold climate, gardeners are unlikely to harvest from the breba crop in late spring.

Hibiscus cooperi—grown for its tri-colored foliage as much as its scarlet red flowers

Hibiscus

(hie-BIS-cuss)

COMMON NAME: Hibiscus

LIGHT: Full sun

NATIVE TO: Temperate, subtropical, and tropical regions worldwide

POTENTIAL PESTS/DISEASE: Deer, aphids, spider mite

GREAT AS A: Summer Romance

Heartbreaker™ Hollywood™ *Hibiscus* sports vivid orange blooms with glossy green foliage and a compact habit. Perfect for containers.

Hibiscus is a curious and beautiful genus, having a foot in both temperate and tropical climates. There are hundreds of hardy *Hibiscus* hybrids bred from species that flourish in marshes and wetlands in many places in the South and Southwestern United States, and whose wide, silky petals and contrasting stamens add an exotic, tropical note to temperate gardens. *H. palustris*, *H. moscheutos*, and *H. coccinea* make up the parentage of many of these hybrids.

Though the foliage on these species is almost as delicate as the flowers, and is beloved by deer and Japanese beetles, gardeners who yearn to create a fully tropical garden would be wise to incorporate some of these Mocktrop hybrids into the mix to make the fall migration less onerous. From the island-red of 'Lord Baltimore,' to the dinner plate–sized pink blooms and coppery foliage of 'Kopper King' they will bloom from late summer till fall on shrubs from 2 to 5 feet (61 cm to 1.5 m) in height. Flowers can be found in almost every color from pink to yellow.

Leathery, sometimes glossy foliage and vivid petals characterize many of the tropical hybrids that are grouped under *H. rosa sinensis* (literally, Chinese rose), but have their roots in up to eight species. Though tender, they are visually sturdier plants or small shrubs/trees and can bloom quite early in the season.

If you question growing tropical species when there are hardy ones, a quick dive into the intense color patterns and flower forms of hybrids like 'Samba Dancer' or 'Voodoo Queen' may be enough to convince you. Or try something exotically different like *H. cooperi,* whose simple leaves are liberally splashed with white, red, and green. Tropical species respond well to pruning and make exceptional container plants for decks, patios, and small gardens.

H. sabdariffa, or roselle, is a popular edible hibiscus that boasts beautiful red calyces once the red-throated white flowers have faded. Dried and boiled in water, the calyces form the basis of many drinks in the Caribbean and Africa. The leaves are eaten as *chin baung ywet,* or sour leaf, in Burmese cuisine.

Ipomoea

(eye-pome-OH-ay-ah)

COMMON NAMES: Sweet potato vine, morning glory vine, batatas, mina

LIGHT: Full sun

NATIVE TO: West Indies, North America, South Africa, and Asia

POTENTIAL PESTS/DISEASE: Sweet potato weevil, aphids, flea beetles

GREAT AS A: Summer Romance

Ipomoea batatas trails gently in a stunning container with papyrus and *Lantana* cultivars.

Multicolored racemes of *Ipomoea lobata* blend the reds and yellows of *Dahlia* and *Rudbeckia* in an autumn border.

Flowering vines bring color, texture, and romance to the summer garden, but few do it as exotically and inexpensively as the genus *Ipomoea*, which contains not only the beloved, if rampant, morning glories (*I. tricolor*), but also edible/ornamental sweet potatoes (*I. batatas*), and unusual, exotic fire vines (*I. lobata*). Many species can be easily reared from seed, some from slips started on overwintered tubers, and others bought cheaply as finished plants for trailing accents in sunny containers.

Once *Ipomoea* have begun to flower, they do so profusely throughout the summer months. Leaves come in many shapes, and in the case of sweet potato vine, are specifically bred for leaf variation. Whether blue, white, red, pink, or iridescent purple, the deep-throated blossoms are very attractive to hummingbirds and pollinators.

Fire vine (*I. lobata*) is a spectacular vining *Ipomoea* for borders and trellises with small tubular flowers that fade from red to orange to yellow to white along long racemes held on dark-red stems. The flowers are held on one side of the stem, and pair perfectly with a late-summer or autumn border. Another easy seed-grown *Ipomoea* is cardinal vine (*I. quamoclit*), which drapes layers of feathery green leaves along trellises and dots them with small crimson red trumpets.

Not all *Ipomoea* are vines. *I. carnea*, the pink morning glory tree, and the perhaps more floriferous white-flowered variety 'Albiflora' can reach upwards of 5 to 6 feet (1.5 to 1.8 m), with characteristic blossoms sometimes too quick to spread seed in warmer climates.

For gardeners who are creating a garden to be enjoyed after the sun sets, moonflower (*I. alba*) is a fascinating, fragrant plant. Its large pure white trumpets open quickly after dusk and roll back up with the return of the sun.

Ipomoea species tend to be very vigorous and can cover a trellis or smother a precious plant. Don't be hesitant with the pruners—your plant will grow back. The trimmings of ornamental sweet potato vine are edible and can be sautéed like spinach; but a new series, Treasure Island®, has been specifically bred to deliver flavor *and* color in tubers and leaves.

Justicia

(juss-TISH-shee-uh)

COMMON NAME: Shrimp plant, Brazilian plume flower

LIGHT: Full sun to shade

NATIVE TO: Tropical and subtropical regions worldwide

POTENTIAL PESTS/DISEASE: Aphids, spider mite

GREAT AS A: Summer Romance

Justicia carnea begins blooming even as a small plant with little sun exposure.

For temperate gardeners who love plants that flower all season in fascinating, unusual ways, and do so in exposures that vary from sun to shade, *Justicia* is a genus to explore, though you are unlikely to come close to experiencing all of the more than 400 species. In general, most species favor moist but well-drained soils and can become quite bushy and dense as semi-shrubs, especially when tip pruned regularly. Foliage varies, but is usually quite attractive in shades of bright to deep green, with deep veining often in purple shades.

Adventurous gardeners are not likely to make a connection with the common name "shrimp plant" until they stand in front of *J. brandegeeana*, whose exotic, drooping spikes of overlapping bracts superficially resemble shrimp tails—both in form and in their orange-pink color. It's one of the most popular species sold at garden centers and is no doubt responsible for more than hundreds of impulse purchases daily. Sun to light shade is preferred.

Digging a little deeper, try the shade-loving *J. carnea*. Large plumes of rose-pink flowers adorn this plant all season, and the foliage of some cultivars can turn quite purple. Two hours of sun seems adequate to keep the blooms coming, bringing welcome color to some of your shadier areas.

J. betonica is another blooming marvel, flowering with tall 6-inch (15-cm) spikes of white bracts deeply traced with green that open to small lavender or pink flowers. The candle-like spikes are held on top of a shrubby, full framework that thrives in sun. A great choice for gardeners trying to attract hummingbirds. Another hummingbird magnet is *J. floribunda* (firecracker flower), but with a different flower form and color. Tubular yellow-tipped orange blossoms hang in clusters against deep green foliage with both large and small ovate leaves.

If you get hold of other rarer species, consider taking cuttings in the fall, as they strike extremely well and grow vigorously. Many species will be root killed at 20°F (-6°C) but sprout again with warm summer temps.

Justicia brandegeeana with its distinctive shrimp-like blooms. (Aldrich Garden, Alexandria, Virginia)

Lantana

(lan-TAN-uh)

COMMON NAMES: Lantana

LIGHT: Full sun, light shade

NATIVE TO: Tropical North, Central, and South America; South Africa

POTENTIAL PESTS/DISEASE: Spider mite, whitefly

GREAT AS A: Best Friend

Lantana in mid-autumn. Here, Hot Blooded® 'Red' and Bandolero™ 'Pineapple.'

When heat indexes rise, *Lantana* greets the gardener with vivid tropical color, blooming reliably for the rest of the season with tiny trumpet flowers produced in domed clusters. Many of the most popular cultivars are multicolored—adding greatly to the appeal. The deer-resistant foliage is serrated, deep green, and has a rough texture.

Lantana cultivars are bred from *both* trailing and mounding species, and have been mightily improved over the last decades, so once you've found the ones you adore, don't go back to the garden center next year and simply ask for "a yellow lantana." Know the names of cultivars and/or series that make you happy.

Cultivars of *Lantana montevidensis,* such as the vigorous purple Luscious® 'Grape,' are trailing, and make great groundcovers or tough companions in a sunny patio container. Full sun is best for all *Lantana*, but they can be grown in light shade if you don't mind a decrease in bloom. They are very forgiving of poor soil conditions and periods of drought.

For more structure, choose cultivars of *L. camara*. Two of my favorite mounding cultivars are: Luscious® 'Bananarama' (yellow) and Hot Blooded® 'Red'—which is fully sterile. The Bandana® series also produces reliable, uniform plants (<24 inches [61 cm]) in seemingly endless color combinations. Another popular cultivar, 'Samantha,' has white and green variegated foliage with yellow blooms, and half sprawls, half mounds in a very pleasing way.

General availability means that *Lantana* make a fine Summer Romance, but if you have found a cultivar you might not see next year at the garden center, dig them and bag them with the rest of your Best Friends. *Lantana* also root well from tip cuttings taken in fall. If you bring your plants into living spaces, be prepared for the worst aspects of a High-Maintenance relationship—spider mites, whitefly, and general winter awkwardness. They are also toxic to pets and children.

The tiny trumpet flowers of *Lantana* are held in clusters and are very attractive to pollinators, such as this hummingbird clearwing moth.

Mandevilla

(man-duh-VILL-uh)

COMMON NAMES: Rock trumpet, dipladenia, mandevilla

LIGHT: Full sun

NATIVE TO: Central and South America

POTENTIAL PESTS/DISEASE: Spider mite, aphids, thrips

GREAT AS A: Summer Romance

Dipladenia has recently become part of the genus *Mandevilla*, and shows off a more compact habit that is wonderful for hanging baskets. (Thanksgiving Farms, Frederick, Maryland)

One of the most recognizable tropical plants at garden centers, *Mandevilla*'s shiny, deep green (and sometimes variegated) leaves, vivid funnel-shaped flowers, and vigorous, vining tendrils have lured more than one tropical newbie into a Summer Romance. Though they can be overwintered as a High-Maintenance Partner indoors, they won't make it easy on the love-struck gardener, and will lose leaves and become a pest magnet if bright, humid conditions are not given to them.

However, with large availability and new and improved cultivars coming out every spring, the gardener might find that a ready-to-go 24-inch (61-cm) Summer Romance at the garden center is sometimes more preferable than one that still needs to put on some clothes after a winter indoors.

Grow *Mandevilla* on a trellis in fertile, well-draining soil that is allowed to dry out slightly before watering. *Mandevilla* has a woody stem and vining tendrils that allow it to move through a trellis and support itself without constant tying in, but it is good to keep nipping and tucking the plant to make sure it's heading the way you want it to. Flowers are borne in groups or racemes at leaf axils, and bloom in pink, white, red, variegated red, and apricot.

For a shorter, bushier plant well suited to hanging baskets, try cultivars labeled *Dipladenia*. Taxonomists now have the genus *Mandevilla* absorbing *Dipladenia*, but old habits die hard and you are likely to see this name still used at garden centers. If you have a favorite, it is much better to remember and look for the cultivar name, as new and old cultivars tend to come to market with no reference to species. The Sundenia® series, Tropic Escape® Costa del Sol series, and 'Summervillea' are all bushy specimens that flower profusely.

'Alice du Pont' is an old but lovely vining cultivar with attractive, wrinkled leaves and pink flowers that is hard to beat. Much larger and smoother leaves characterize the Sun Parasol® Giant series—the green and white leaves and scarlet blossoms of 'Giant Marbled Crimson' are extremely striking in a large container.

Sun Parasol® Giant Dark Pink *Mandevilla* in mid-summer

Bananas (Musaceae)

GENERA DISCUSSED: *Ensete, Musa*

LIGHT: Full sun to part shade

NATIVE TO: Northeast India, Southeast Asia, Australia, Japan, tropical regions of Africa

POTENTIAL PESTS/DISEASE: Spider mite, aphids, Japanese beetles

GREAT AS A: High-Maintenance Partner

Musa 'Ae Ae' is an exciting cultivar with standout variegated foliage.

The impact of a stately banana tree in a garden is undeniable. They can create an instant architectural feature—particularly valuable to a young garden. With plenty of sun, water, and fertilizer over the season, your banana will continuously unfurl wide, exotic leaves from a growing point in the center of a single stem

Bananas can tolerate partial shade conditions, but will bend slightly toward the light and be less robust. For all bananas, a sheltered space from wind is preferable, as tender young leaves will shred. However, if you don't have those conditions, grow bananas anyway and embrace the look of the islands.

Whether *Musa* or *Ensete* species (and except for the hardy banana, *M. basjoo*, hardy to -10°F [-23°C]), bananas must be dug and brought into a basement, garage, or greenhouse over the winter. Do not expect to get fruit unless you can keep the banana in active growth. In the case of *M. basjoo* (where it is hardy) you may choose to wrap the entire stem in a cocoon of protective materials to allow fruiting for the next year. Many gardeners choose instead to cut the plant to the ground and mulch heavily, creating a clump of new stems that are grown only for foliage. *Musa itinerans* 'Mekong Giant' is reported to share hardiness to 0°F (-18°C) with the added ornamentation of red, striated stems.

Once bananas flower and fruit, the plant dies. In *Musa* species, new "pups" will have formed and can be separated with a sharp knife. *Ensete* will not pup unless the growing tip has been severely damaged.

The red Abyssinian banana (*E. ventricosum* 'Maurelii') is a popular choice for its deep red-green leaves that are some of the widest in banana species.

Summer rain and *Musa acuminata* 'Ice Cream'—a perfect combination

Above *Musa basjoo* accenting an otherwise temperate bed. (Zimmermann-Roberts Garden, Brunswick, Maryland)

Left *Ensete ventricosum* 'Maurelii' add color and strong architectural lines to this tropical planting. (Chanticleer Garden, Wayne, Pennsylvania)

M. acuminata 'Ice Cream' boasts creamy green stems and leaves, and *M. balbisiana* 'Black Thai' will deliver shock and awe with black glossy stems. Less hardy *Musa* species have a slimmer profile than broad-leafed *Ensete*, but this allows the gardener to paint with colorful, tall foliage accents without dominating the picture. 'Siam Ruby' is a striking orange-leafed cultivar with dapples of green—'Ae Ae' a variegated hybrid with pronounced creamy stripes. Along a pathway, the reddening undersides of the red-striped *M. sikkmensis* 'Bengal Tiger' will have an even greater effect.

Dwarf hybrids such as *M.* x 'Dwarf Cavendish' or 'Truly Tiny' often sport red stippling on green leaves. At a smaller size of 6 feet (1.8 m), you might just try one for some fruit indoors!

The leaves of *Musa* and *Ensete* species can be used as food wrappers for many dishes, from tamales to broiled fish. In Ethiopia, pulp is extracted from the leaves of *Ensete* and fermented to create a starchy food staple as an insurance against hunger.

Nephrolepis

(ne-froh-LEP-is)

COMMON NAMES: Sword fern, Boston fern, Kimberley queen fern, macho fern

LIGHT: Shade to part sun to full sun

NATIVE TO: Tropical Americas and Africa

POTENTIAL PESTS/DISEASE: Japanese beetles, spider mite

GREAT AS A: Summer Romance

Kimberley queen fern (*N. obliterata*) with sweet potato vine and wax begonias

Hanging Boston ferns (*N. exaltata*) typify gracious Southern charm.

Temperate gardeners have a lot of choices when it comes to hardy garden ferns, but few are as suited to hanging baskets, urns, and other containers as the tender *Nephrolepis* species. From the charming delicacy of Boston ferns (*N. exaltata* 'Bostoniensis') to the leathery brute strength of macho ferns (*N. falcata*), their mounding habit and vigorous seasonal growth set them apart as a must-buy for many gardeners seeking luxurious foliage accents for a shade to part-shade garden.

The fronds of *Nephrolepis* species are often uniformly sword-shaped, leading to this genus's most commonly used name, but species and cultivars can display fascinating variations. In general, the waxier the pinnae (individual leaves on fronds), the more sun the species will tolerate and the more tolerant they are of the absent-minded waterer. Repotting a *Nephrolepis* into a larger pot will help with its water requirements, as the plants are almost always root-bound when you buy them from a garden center. In areas with milder summers, you'll find most *Nephrolepis* can cope with more sun without burning.

Boston ferns are the best known of the genus, with softly mounding fronds that instantly invoke the feeling of gracious Southern gardens. 'Bostoniensis Blue Bell' has shorter fronds, brighter green color, and a ball-like appearance. 'Golden Boston' is a chartreuse cultivar of the species.

As they are extremely vigorous and lush, sword ferns work well as stand-alone plants in containers. I have had a quart-size Kimberley queen (*N. obliterata*) completely fill a whiskey barrel in a season, and a macho send runners out of its sizable container and into a neighboring pot before I could catch it. In the landscape, they will attempt to run and can be invasive, but winters below 20°F (-6°C) ensure the gardener's victory over those wiry roots.

Other fun species/cultivars to try: Lemon button fern (*N. cordifolia* 'Duffi') with small fronds and a whiff of lemony scent. Fishtail fern (*N. falcata* 'Furcans') with crested pinnae that resemble fish tails.

Indoors, *Nephrolepis* are not for the faint of heart, as they need humidity, high indoor light, and regular moisture or they will drop pinnae like a flower girl at a wedding. If the pot is on the small side, I usually bring them in as a temporary indoor foliage accent until we're both sick of each other.

Peperomia

(pep-er-OH-mee-uh)

COMMON NAMES: Peperomia, radiator plant

LIGHT: Shade to light sun

NATIVE TO: Subtropical and tropical regions worldwide

POTENTIAL PESTS/DISEASE: Mealy bug and mites; quite resistant to pests

GREAT AS A: Long-Term Commitment

The strong, waxy leaves and intense variegation of *Peperomia obtusifolia* 'Variegata'.

Peperomia graveolens is a particularly succulent species.

Peperomia is a diverse genus of more than 1,000 species that could make you forget about your outside garden and turn you into a houseplant collector. From the puckered, red-stemmed foliage of *P. caperata* to the rolled, lanceolate leaves of *P. ferreyrae*, there is a *Peperomia* for every taste. Some trail, some mound, some spread, and others grow upright, but all have a fairly shallow root system, and can absorb moisture through their leaves.

Using *Peperomia* species as Long-Term Commitments makes a great deal of sense: the plants enjoy higher humidity levels in the summer months, and coloration in many of the variegated species (such as the waxy-leaved *P. obtusifolia* 'Variegata') becomes more prominent in higher light conditions. However, *Peperomia* should not be put in full sun. They prefer shade to light shade and can easily scorch. In late summer, some species will show just how happy they are by flowering with alienesque spikes or bottlebrushes held just above the foliage.

P. clusiifolia 'Variegata' is another variegated peperomia with more elongated leaves tinged with red. The watermelon peperomia (*P. argyreia*) is a marbled glossy-leaved stunner that strongly resembles watermelon rind and is a great choice for a hanging basket.

Peperomia are easily propagated through division or leaf or stem cuttings, particularly during the summer months, and pruning to keep growth neat is recommended if you are planning on bringing them indoors in the fall. Do so before the frost falls, as *Peperomia* are extremely sensitive. Indoors, keep water to a minimum, hold off on fertilizer, and grow in a medium to bright situation.

Peperomia are not large houseplants, and the best use for them outside is tucked in corners, hanging baskets, and containers where their foliage makes the most impact.

Several species/cultivars of *Peperomia* can allow you to have the classic 'succulent trough' look, even if you don't have full sun. To get started, try *P. axillaris* and *P. graveolens*, paired with the shade-tolerant sedum *S. ternatum*.

Philodendron

(fill-oh-DEN-dron)

COMMON NAME: Philodendron

LIGHT: Shade to light shade

NATIVE TO: Tropical Americas, West Indies

POTENTIAL PESTS/DISEASE: Aphids, mealy bug, Southern blight

GREAT AS A: Long-Term Commitment

Philodendron 'McColley's Finale'

Philodendron are one of the first houseplants we take on as eager plantparents. They are tolerant of lower light levels and a forgetful caretaker, and grace indoor spaces with many different shapes. However, taken outside in summer to a sheltered spot in the garden or patio, they will greatly benefit from increased moisture, humidity, and light levels, and will come back inside with a new lease on life.

The wide variation in species and cultivars is perhaps better understood if you categorize them into three distinct groups: vining/climbing, self-heading, and erect-arborescent.

Those in the vining/climbing group are easy to grow, and show off classic heart- to arrow-shaped leaves that even non-gardeners recognize as *Philodendron*. They are grown to best advantage in hanging baskets or climbing up a moss-covered pole to reawaken their origins as tree-scramblers in the tropics. In addition to basic green species, or those with yellow variegation, look out for *P. brandtianum* with silver leaves marked with green veins.

Philodendron hederaceum 'Brasil' in a west-facing window

The self-heading group brings lush, colorful foliage into our living rooms, with large erect leaves that unfurl in shades of orange, red, chartreuse, and deep purple, and then frame newer foliage as they revert to deeper colors. They are used to best effect in the landscape by plunging the pots into contrasting foliage in shady sites—or creating a tropical shrub effect by using a few together. They can be a little more temperamental than vining types—do not saturate them. Try *P.* 'Moonlight,' 'McColley's Finale,' or 'Rojo Congo.' 'Birkin' is a new cultivar with striking green-on-white variegation.

Given enough time, erect-arborescent *Philodendron* can slowly become tree-like in a corner, but resemble self-heading types until that "trunk" is created. The journey is an attractive one, and many sport fabulously lobed or frilled leathery leaves on the ends of strong petioles. Some are soil-hardy to 20°F (-6°C). *P. selloum* is one of the best known of this group, and 'Hope' is one of its hardiest cultivars (at least 10°F [-9°C]). These *Philodendron* can tolerate more sun and will start to reach in deep shade.

Plectranthus

(plek-TRAN-thus)

COMMON NAMES: Spurflower, coleus

LIGHT: Shade to sun

NATIVE TO: Africa, Asia, Pacific Islands, Australasia, Madagascar

POTENTIAL PESTS/DISEASE: Mealy bug, spider mite, stem rot

GREAT AS A: Summer Romance or High-Maintenance Partner

Silver-leaved *Plectranthus argentatus* nestled between *Xanthosoma aurea* 'Lime Zinger' and white wax *Begonia*

The genus *Plectranthus* has now absorbed one of North America's favorite annuals—coleus—but even without this colorful group of foliage plants, the genus has plenty to offer the temperate gardener gardening in shade or sun. They mound, they trail, and they dazzle—a versatile genus that adds much to a container or garden bed.

Though there are variations in leaf shape, *Plectranthus* leaves are usually ovate or round and the margins are somewhat serrated or scalloped, with an inherent softness in many species that is often due to a network of fine hairs. Some are highly fragrant—like Cuban oregano (*P. amboinicus*). Stems are square, and provide lots of nooks and crannies for mealy bug—one of their worst enemies.

Species and cultivars within *Plectranthus* vary in their ability to tolerate sun. In my experience, even sun-loving species like the silvery-gray *P. argentatus* are happiest when somewhat sheltered from hot afternoon rays. Most prefer a shade or part-shade situation.

Whether dealing with your favorite coleus hybrid ('Gay's Delight' and the FlameThrower™ series for me!), or a trailing *Plectranthus* such as *P. forsteri* 'Marginatus,' all plants benefit from regular pinching to promote fullness.

Plectranthus species bloom in racemes of two-lipped flowers at the ends of stems. Some flowers are a bonus to an already beautiful plant—as in the case of the hybrid 'Mona Lavender,' which blooms in late summer/early fall against deep green leaves with an even deeper purple underside. Others are better removed (as with coleus), to promote foliage growth.

Use *Plectranthus* in containers for body, or as trailing accents, allowing them to gently fill empty space in garden beds. Plants showing signs of bleaching or burn are better off with more shade. Many *Plectranthus* species are root hardy to 20°F (-6°C) in the garden.

Indoors, *Plectranthus* needs high light or they become leggy and preyed upon by pests. I prefer to take cuttings of my favorites and root them in water on my windowsill, buying myself time before I have to pot them up in the New Year.

Some *Plectranthus* are grown for both foliage and flower. Here, the fall blooming cultivar 'Mona Lavender.'

A tender white blossom of *Plumeria rubra* displays a silken yellow throat. (Dronenburg/Weil Garden, Knoxville, Maryland)

Plumeria

(ploo-MARE-ee-uh)

COMMON NAME: Frangipani

LIGHT: Full sun

NATIVE TO: Central and South America

POTENTIAL PESTS/DISEASE: Spider mite, aphids

GREAT AS A: Best Friend

Plumeria are architectural plants, even at a young age. Though it will not bloom this year, this juvenile plant is healthy and happy and makes a lovely container specimen.

Seductive yet sacred, *Plumeria* is revered worldwide as a symbol of love, joy, and welcome. It is one of the main blossoms used in Hawaiian leis and its strong architectural presence can be found in the courtyards of Buddhist temples throughout Southeast Asia. It is a small tree of distinction, sometimes as wide as it is tall. Long, gray-brown stems are topped with leathery, veined leaves creating an umbrella effect. As each leaf falls, a pronounced scar remains on the stem.

Plumeria bloom in fragrant, five-petaled flowers of pink, yellow, white, and red that are held on clusters at the ends of stems. They relish sunlight and regular watering, but should not be kept wet.

Despite all this glamour, *Plumeria* can be stored, quietly and easily, as a Best Friend in a frost-free, dark location in winter, taking advantage of the plant's natural dormancy during the dry season. Whether deciduous or evergreen (there are both), it will lose its leaves; but left in its pot and checked occasionally to ensure it is not bone dry, the plant will rejuvenate in the spring when returned to heat, moisture, and a sunny location. For this reason, it is often easiest to keep *Plumeria* containerized—slowly increasing pot size as a tree matures. If you do plant *Plumeria* in the soil, dig the root ball and store using the bagged method for Best Friends (page 55).

Cuttings can be taken in early spring while *Plumeria* is still dormant. Allow them to callus over, then plant in rich soil and water lightly. Later when well rooted, feed with a fertilizer that leans toward a higher level of phosphorus for strong blossoming.

P. rubra is one of the most common garden center species, with pointed, ovate leaves and cultivars in many flower colors with recurved petals—often with throats suffused in a contrasting hue. It is a naturally deciduous species. The evergreen leaves of *P. obtusa* are rounded and shinier, with blossoms of pink or white. In a greenhouse over 60°F (16°C) or indoor setting over the winter, the leaves will remain.

Truly, a tropical plant for the romantic in you.

Sansevieria

(san-se-VEER-ree-uh)

COMMON NAMES: Mother-in-law's tongue, snake plant

LIGHT: Sun, shade

NATIVE TO: Tropical and Subtropical India, Indonesia, Madagascar, Africa

POTENTIAL PESTS/DISEASE: Spider mite and mealy bugs (rare, but possible)

GREAT AS A: Long-Term Commitment

Sansevieria trifasciata 'Laurentii' is the focal point in this colorful container for a partially shaded patio. (Garden of Kellie O'Brien, Chicago, Illinois)

Vertical, variegated accents don't come much easier than *Sansevieria*—a plant that's extremely forgiving of low-light and water conditions and has few pest issues. *Sansevieria* are stemless plants whose fleshy upright leaves grow thickly from spreading rhizomes just underneath the soil's surface. Leaves are often sword-like and flat, but some species may have cylindrical leaves or smaller, ovate leaves held in attractive rosettes.

Most have some degree of variegation, and/or strong margination, and gardeners can choose between the warmer tones of a common cultivar such as *S. trifasciata* 'Laurentii' with golden edges overlaying a banded leaf, or pick up on cooler tones present in the gray bands of *S. zeylanica* or in the shimmering gray leaves of *S. trifasciata* 'Moonshine.' One series of small bird's nest–type *Sansevieria*, Starpower®, comes in ten gorgeous cultivars and is perfect for smaller arrangements.

Thought of as a low-light houseplant, *Sansevieria* are actually grown in full sun and transitioned to shadier conditions before growers ship them to retail outlets. Take advantage of their strong architectural structure and plunge them, pot and all, into the middle of a lush bed of ferns, or tease apart the rhizomes and roots of an overgrown pot and add several pieces to new containers by planting shallowly in a mix of two-thirds potting soil to one-third grit. Fan out the roots and clip off splaying leaves, whose weight can pull the new plant out of the soil. If your plant is heading somewhere sunny, transition it there slowly.

At least three weeks before your last frost, pull up plunged pots and re-plunge them indoors in a prettier container, or repot completely. The clean lines of *Sansevieria* add so much to indoor spaces with so little work on your part, it'll be hard not to make a Long-Term Commitment to this versatile plant.

There have been taxonomic rumblings that *Sansevieria* will eventually become part of the genus *Dracaena*. At the time of press, horticulturists weren't changing their plant tags, but it's worth keeping in mind.

This is why taxonomists have a hard time getting invited to garden parties.

The strong silver banding of *S. zeylanica* makes it the perfect partner for gray-and-white-themed containers and beds.

Schefflera

(chef-LEER-uh)

COMMON NAME: Umbrella tree

LIGHT: Full sun to part shade

NATIVE TO: Southeast Asia, Central and South America

POTENTIAL PESTS/DISEASE: Scale, mites, occasional leaf spot

GREAT AS A: Long-Term Commitment

Schefflera makes a bold foliage statement inside, and is relatively easy to keep happy during the long months of winter. Its leaves are made up of several leaflets held on long petioles attached to woody stems. Species commonly found in garden centers and grocery stores are *S. arboricola*—with smaller leaves, often variegated, and *S. actinophylla*, a stately tree with large, 8- to 12-inch (20- to 30-cm) leaves that make a big impact in a living room or in a large, bright bathroom.

A shiny *Schefflera* is a happy *Schefflera*. If you're not watering too frequently and feeding regularly, try adjusting the level of sunlight down a little to achieve peak shine. Most plants of the above species are sold as several stems in a pot—creating a shrub-like effect; but given time, *S. actinophylla* can grow to be a stately tree. *S. arboricola* is widely used as a hedge plant in tropical regions of the world. Both *S. actinophylla* and *S. arboricola* have some degree of salt tolerance and therefore make great deck or patio plants for coastal locations.

S. elegantissima (false aralia) is a highly ornamental, textured species of *Schefflera*. The purple/black leaflets are thin, feathery, and serrated, and the plant makes a delicate accent against wide green foliage in the garden. It is sensitive to underwatering and will lose leaves quickly if allowed to dry out severely. Variegated cultivars 'Galaxy,' 'Bianca,' and 'Gold Crest' make extremely attractive houseplants as their wider, serrated leaves are edged with cream or golden tones.

Those gardening in climates with winters above 5°F (-15°C) can leave *S. delavayi* outside in a sheltered position. It's a slow-growing, fairly hardy *Schefflera* with serrated wide leaflets and makes an attractive shrub where it isn't cut back to the ground each winter.

Schefflera require regular moisture during a hot summer, but once indoors for the winter, it is better that the plant be kept on the dry side, so roots do not rot. Place it in a bright situation inside, and rotate it frequently to maintain shape.

Schefflera arboricola enjoying a summer vacation with *S. actinophylla*, *Strelitzia nicolai*, and *Ficus elastica*

S. elegantissima against a backdrop of *Canna* 'Bengal Tiger'

Strelitzia

(strell-LITZ-ee-uh)

COMMON NAME: Bird of paradise

LIGHT: Full sun to light shade

NATIVE TO: South Africa

POTENTIAL PESTS/DISEASE: Scale

GREAT AS A: Long-Term Commitment

Regal *Strelitzia reginae* against a mimosa backdrop

It's taken many years for me to find *Strelitzia* attractive—and I credit my change of heart to the online plant parents who have showed it to best advantage inside their homes. My shocking prejudice is due to many years in Southern California, where along with *Agapanthus*, it is overplanted like an East Coast magenta azalea. Familiarity breeds contempt.

However, in colder regions of the world, its upright leathery leaves and flamboyant orange and blue blooms are prized—particularly as they tend to flower from autumn to spring indoors. I have come to view it as an architectural plant, slowly unfurling tough, sometimes glaucous leaves at jaunty angles. I even see the occasional deep tear as artistic, and enjoy using the plant as an anchor on my deck.

Strelitzia has a tropical appearance—both indoors and out—but actually comes from a drier, more Mediterranean climate. It can handle moisture if soil is well drained and the rhizomes are not planted too deeply—plant at the surface of the soil. The flowers appear after the plant has attained some level of maturity—sometimes as long as seven years—petals and sepals blending together to form the magnificently shaped head and bill of an exotic large bird. Blooms are very long lasting and are of high value in bouquets.

There are five species of *Strelitzia*, most of which are quite tall—to 30 feet (9.1 m) in warm climates. The white-flowered *S. nicolai* is only just getting started at 4 feet (1.2 m), so it's important to think ahead before you impulse buy. For the most part, the average gardener with average space looking for the best characteristics of the genus will be very satisfied with the smaller-leafed cultivars of *S. reginae*, which top out at 6 feet (1.8 m), including the variety 'Humilis,' which is further dwarfed. *S. juncea* is a fascinating smaller species whose long, un-leafed petioles resemble rushes. If you can find it, grab it!

Repotting your *Strelitzia* when it feels crowded can stop it flowering. Let it go longer between re-pottings and increase pot size gradually.

Clumps of *Strelitzia* foliage can make strong statements in the garden, but this is a tropical plant grown mostly for its exquisite flowers.

Gingers
(Zingiberaceae)

GENERA DISCUSSED: *Alpinia, Zingiber, Hedychium, Curcuma, Cautleya, Roscoea*

LIGHT: Part shade to sun

NATIVE TO: Subtropical and tropical regions worldwide

POTENTIAL PESTS/DISEASE: Remarkably pest resistant

GREAT AS A: Best Friend or High Maintenance Partner

A family for cooks and plant collectors, gingers are an aromatic, visually arresting group of fifty genera and hundreds of species, but unless you're a collector with a greenhouse, you are likely to see only a handful of those species in garden centers—and indeed, your grocery store. Turmeric (*Curcuma longa*) and culinary ginger (*Zingiber officinale*) are both members—as well as the high-contrast foliage plant, variegated shell ginger (*Alpinia zerumbet* 'Variegata'). Gingers prefer moist and often partially shaded conditions, depending on the strength of your sunshine.

In temperate climates, gardeners will be challenged by the ginger family—though this should not stop you from working with them. Even if you cannot get your plant to flower (many will never flower in a temperate climate), the foliage is fascinating, the stems, architectural, and if grown through an artificially extended temperate season, sun-loving culinary species such as *Curcuma longa* and *Zingiber officinale* can have their young rhizomes harvested for the kitchen.

I think it's important to devote a few words to storage. Although gingers spread through rhizomes similar to *Canna*, if they are stored dormant as Best Friends, they do not instantly wake up like *Canna*, and need a prolonged period of warmer temperatures (almost thirty days) to trigger growth. New "seed" rhizomes also benefit from being allowed to

Hedychium coccineum 'Tara'

sprout in a warm place with a light covering of soil until they get going, then planted more deeply. This means starting early and keeping warmth and moisture consistent. They are very susceptible to rot.

Ideally, gingers tend to do better if the rhizomes are undisturbed. These are good candidates for keeping potted in stasis in a lit, cool garage, and plunging into the garden for the season (healthy rhizomes can break pots, so go big!); or create the warmest microclimates you can for hardier species that flower well, such as the early-flowering *Curcuma zedoaria* (hidden ginger) (5°F [-15°C]), which displays a distinctive red stripe down the midvein of each leaf.

Curcuma zedoaria
(Photo credit: Steve Owens)

Mulched in a sheltered, warm location, hardy *Hedychium* species such as *H. coronarium* (5°F [-15°C]), *H. coccineum* (0°F [-18°C]), or *H. densiflorum* (0°F [-18°C]) may not emerge until early summer—but if the season stays warm and the water is flowing, you should have fragrant, magnificent panicles of blossom by season's end. Other species with tremendous hardiness are the yellow- and red-flowered *Cautleya spicata* (0°F [-18°C]), and the almost orchid, almost iris, uncomfortably risqué species of *Roscoea* (-10°F [-23°C]). The latter prefers a drier soil.

If you don't want to fiddle with storage issues, but wish to go beyond a Summer Romance relationship *and* your winter temperatures don't dip below -10°F (-23°C), try the vigorous and vertical Japanese ginger (*Zingiber mioga*), especially the attractive variegated form 'Dancing Crane.' The late-season blossoms emerge at soil level and are a delicacy in Japanese cuisine.

Don't Let Them Get Away

There's never enough room when you're writing a book, but I can't let these
stunning plants go without a mention. . . .

MANIHOT ESCULENTA 'VARIEGATA' (VARIEGATED TAPIOCA)

Exotic, yet delicate, the palmate yellow and green leaves of variegated tapioca are held on thin coral petioles attached to reddening stems. Whether grown as a 5-foot (1.5-m) specimen or as a small container darling, it is simply stunning in a sunny location, and root hardy down to 10° to 15°F (1- to -9°C).

CISSUS DISCOLOR (REX BEGONIA VINE)

Rex begonia vine has nothing to do with a rex begonia, but the long heart-shaped burgundy leaves streaked with white are strongly reminiscent of its namesake. Grow this vigorous vine in rich soil in shade. Pots can be brought in and overwintered as Best Friends but need heat to break their slumber in spring.

Manihot esculenta 'Variegata'

Cissus discolor with autumn fern (*Dryopteris erythrosora*)

SANCHEZIA NOBILIS (SANCHEZIA)

A horticulturist friend who has worked with tropical plants for many years once listed *Sanchezia* as his number one foliage plant. That's saying something. Shiny green 5- to 10-inch (13- to 25-cm) leaves are deeply veined with bright yellow, and if overwintered as a High-Maintenance Partner, this plant will slowly grow into an impressive shrub that sports yellow flowers with reddish bracts. Sun to part shade. Keep it moist.

Sanchezia nobilis

PTERIS CRETICA 'ALBO-LINEATA' (CRETAN BRAKE FERN)

Pteris cretica 'Albo-lineata'

Brake ferns add a delicate touch of exoticism to any container, but the white-on-green fronds of *P. cretica 'Albo-lineata'* are simply magical. Grow it in partial shade in rich, well-draining soil—and consider giving it a terrarium in winter to showcase the grace indoors.

APHELANDRA SQUARROSA (ZEBRA PLANT)

Zebra plant is a strong foliage plant for shady situations outdoors, and an excellent Long-Term Commitment for those who find themselves entranced by its deep green leaves veined and ribbed in creamy white. Moist, rich soils are preferred, and zebra plant can deal well with lower light levels. Yellow flowers are a bonus for a plant that looks great throughout the year.

Aphelandra squarrosa

Coprosma 'Tequila Sunrise'

COPROSMA REPENS (MIRROR BUSH)

For those in climates with winters above 20°F (-6°C), the colorful, shiny, and heat-tolerant foliage of *Coprosma* is probably familiar, and breeders have been doing miraculous things with new cultivars of this smaller-leafed shrub. *Coprosma* can be grown as a High-Maintenance Partner in strong light without too much difficulty. Full sun to light shade. Cuttings root well.

EUPHORBIA MILII (CROWN OF THORNS)

To these (primarily) foliage plants I add one you should grow specifically for its flowers—indoors and out—for they never stop. The flowers of crown of thorns are actually colored bracts, in shades of pink, salmon, yellow, white, and orange; but it's the spiny stems that give this *Euphorbia* its common name. Cut back stems occasionally to keep it bushy, and mind the white sap that immediately oozes—it is irritating to skin. Sun to part shade, very heat- and drought-tolerant, and happy in poor soils. Variegated foliage cultivars are available.

STROBILANTHES DYERIANUS (PERSIAN SHIELD)

The iridescent silvery-purple foliage of Persian shield allows it to pair easily and spectacularly with traditional container plants—particularly the silvers of *Artemisia*, dusty miller, or *Eucalyptus*. It's a subtropical, sun to part-sun plant that's easy to get, easy to grow, and yet still feels highly unusual. Use as a Summer Romance in climates with winters above 20°F (-6°C), or turn your hand to cuttings in the fall—Persian shield roots quickly.

Iridescent Persian shield with a violet *Calibrachoa*

Euphorbia milii plunged into the landscape for the season

Resources and Further Exploration

RETAIL AND MAIL ORDER NURSERIES

Bird Rock Tropicals
Encinitas, California, USA
www.birdrocktropicals.com

Black Olive East Nursery
Fort Lauderdale, Florida, USA
www.blackoliveeastnursery.net

Botanical Growers (Ken's Philodendrons, UrbanTropicals)
Hampton, Florida, USA
www.urbantropicals.com /
www.kensphilodendrons.com

Brian's Botanicals
Louisville, Kentucky, USA
www.briansbotanicals.net

Bromeliad.com
Englewood, Florida, USA
www.bromeliad.com

Bustani Plant Farm
Stillwater, Oklahoma, USA
www.bustaniplantfarm.com

Cistus Nursery
Portland, Oregon, USA
www.cistus.com

Dancing Oaks Nursery Gardens
Monmouth, Oregon, USA
www.dancingoaks.com

Far Reaches Farm
Port Townsend, Washington, USA
www.farreachesfarm.com

Kartuz Greenhouse
Vista, California, USA
www.kartuz.com

Logee's
Danielson, Connecticut, USA
www.logees.com

Michael's Bromeliads
Venice, Florida, USA
www.michaelsbromeliads.com

Plant Delights
Raleigh, North Carolina, USA
www.plantdelights.com

Plant Oddities
Paducah, Kentucky, USA
www.plantoddities.com

Rainforest Flora, Inc.
Torrance, California, USA
www.rainforestflora.com

Top Tropicals
Ft. Myers, Florida, USA
www.toptropicals.com

SEED SUPPLIERS

Baker Creek Heirloom Seeds
Mansfield, Missouri, USA
www.rareseeds.com

Chiltern Seeds
Wallingford, Oxfordshire, UK
www.chilternseeds.co.uk

GeoSeed
Hodges, South Carolina, USA
www.geoseed.com

Hawaii Clean Seed, LLC
Pahoa, Hawaii, USA
www.hawaiianorganicginger.com

Kitazawa Seeds, Oakland CA
Oakland, California, USA
www.kitazawaseed.com

Onalee's Seeds, LLC
Madeira Beach, Florida, USA
www.onalee.com

Rare Palm Seeds
München, Germany
www.rarepalmseeds.com

Silverhill Seeds
Cape Town, South Africa
www.silverhillseeds.co.za

Steve's Leaves
Lewisville, Texas, USA
www.stevesleaves.com

Strictly Medicinal Seeds
Williams, Oregon, USA
www.strictlymedicinalseeds.com

Thompson & Morgan
Ipswich, Suffolk, UK
www.thompson-morgan.com

Tradewinds Fruit
Santa Rosa, California, USA
www.tradewindsfruit.com

FURTHER EXPLORATION

Baggett, Pam. *Tropicalismo!* Portland, Oregon: Timber Press, 2008.

Branney, T.M.E. *Hardy Gingers.* Portland, Oregon: Timber Press, 2005.

Chin, Wee Yeow. *Ferns of the Tropics.* Portland, Oregon: Timber Press, 1997.

Cooke, Ian. *The Gardener's Guide to Growing Cannas.* Portland, Oregon: Timber Press, 2001.

Davidson, John A., Ph.D, and Michael J. Raupp, Ph.D. *Managing Insects and Mites on Woody Plants: An IPM Approach.* 2nd ed. Londonderry, NH: Tree Care Industry Association, 2010.

Giles, Will. *Encyclopedia of Exotic Plants for Temperate Climates.* Portland, Oregon: Timber Press, 2007.

Griffith Jr., Lynn P. *Tropical Foliage Plants: A Grower's Guide.* 2nd ed. Batavia, Illinois: Ball Publishing, 2006.

Hemsley, Alan. *Tropical Garden Style with Hardy Plants.* Lewes, United Kingdom: Guild of Master Craftsman Publications Ltd., 2002.

Hicks, Tom. *Tropical Plant Resource.* Hilton Head Island, South Carolina: Lydia Inglett Ltd., 2013.

Iveren, Richard R. *The Exotic Garden.* Newtown, Connecticut: The Taunton Press, 1999.

Kingsbury, Noël. *Bold and Exotic Plants.* New York: Watson-Guptill Publications, 2000.

Kramer, Jack. *Bromeliads.* New York: Harper & Row, 1981.

Lloyd, Christopher, et al. *Exotic Planting for Adventurous Gardeners.* Portland, Oregon: Timber Press, 2007.

MacCubbin, Tom. *Gardening in Florida.* Nashville, Tennessee: Cool Springs, 2005.

Martin, Byron E. and Laurelynn. *Growing Tasty Tropical Plants.* North Adams, Massachusetts: Storey Publishing, 2010.

National Geographic. *Edible: An Illustrated Guide to the World's Food Plants.* Lane Cove, Australia: Global Book Publishing, 2008.

Preissel, Ulrike and Hans-Georg. *Brugmansia and Datura: Angel's Trumpets and Thorn Apples.* Stuttgart, Germany: Firefly Books, 1997.

Roth, Susan A., and Dennis Schrader. *Hot Plants for Cool Climates: Gardening with Tropical Plants in Temperate Zones.* New York. Houghton Mifflin Company, 2000.

Stewart, Lynette. *A Guide to Palms & Cycads of the World.* Sydney, Australia: Angus & Robertson, 1994.

Thompson, Mildred, and Edward J. Thompson. *Begonias: The Complete Reference Guide.* New York: Times Books, 1981.

Walker, Jacqueline. *The Subtropical Garden.* Portland, Oregon: Timber Press, 1992.

Walls, Ian G. *The Complete Book of the Greenhouse.* 4th ed. London: Cassell & Co., 2001.

Zachos, Ellen. *Tempting Tropicals: 175 Irresistible Indoor Plants.* Portland, Oregon: Timber Press, 2005.

Acknowledgments

With a grateful heart I wish to thank horticulturist, nursery owner, and landscape designer Sylvia Gordon. Her tireless efforts to introduce Northern gardeners to the incredible diversity of plants in her beloved state of Florida were invaluable to this project.

And to my editor, Jessica Walliser, and the excellent team at Quarto, who with a gentle touch and an encouraging word helped me bring this book to fruition in the midst of great challenges.

Also, to the many marvelous gardeners, designers, botanists, researchers, foodies, writers, photographers, horticulturists, breeders, nursery owners, tropical plant enthusiasts, and just plain serious plant people listed below, who allowed me to pick their brains, tour and photograph their gardens, mine their connections, quiz them mercilessly, and sometimes, text them far too late in the evening: Ed Aldrich, Tony Avent, Dan Benarcik, Scott Beuerlein, Peggy Bier, Diane Blasek, John Boggan, Suzanne Boom, Cynthia Brown, Andrew Bunting, Debra DeMarco, Janet Draper, Jim Dronenburg, Irvin Etienne, James Fisk, Fergus Garrett, Andrea Gasper, Pamela Harper, Chad Harrison, Dr. Robert Hartman, Brent Heath, Sara Juarez, Barbara Katz, Panayoti Kelaidis, Brian Killingsworth, Al Maas, Mike Mens, David Muns, Kathy Musial, Jennifer Nelis, Kellie O'Brien, Steve Owens, Gail Pabst, Tom Peace, Bill Pinkham, Linda Pinkham, Kevin Prall, Linda Reindl, Riz Reyes, Michael Rinck, Tamara Risken, Jamee Robinson, Dan Scott, Karen Sparrow, Sandy Stein, Kelly Stevens, Anthony Tesselaar, Bill Thomas, Rob Walser and Allison Walser, Janessa Walsh, John Willis, Lindie Wilson, Ellen Zachos, Mike Zajic, Maria Zampini, Allison Zeeb, Louisa Zimmermann-Roberts, and the hardworking, generous team at the Florida Nursery, Growers and Landscape Association (FNGLA).

To each and every one of you and to those I have inadvertently omitted, thank you for allowing me to use your varied and expert understanding of tropical and subtropical plants in order to help others gain proficiency and confidence in growing them. Your work—in its many forms—is inspiring. —MW

About the Author

Marianne Willburn is a gardening columnist, speaker, and author of *Big Dreams, Small Garden* (2017).

A writer at GardenRant, and a regular contributor to *Better Homes & Gardens*, *The American Gardener*, and other national gardening blogs and magazines, Marianne has also been a mid-Atlantic newspaper columnist for over a decade and is the recipient of several Silver and Gold Media Awards from Garden Communicators International (formerly GWA) for her column.

She gardens in a rural corner of Northern Virginia, working with an ever-evolving mixture of tropical, temperate, and native plants, and shares her gardening life each week on www.smalltowngardener.com.

Index